MEEK AS A MUSTANG

TYNDALE
MOMENTUM™

A Tyndale nonfiction imprint

There's a prophetic edge to Ryan Miller's voice for our present age. His words are honest, timely, loving, confronting, and deeply needed.

MEGAN FATE MARSHMAN, author of *Relaxed*, speaker, teaching pastor at Willow Creek Community Church

Our culture trains us to equate strength with self-assertion, but the gospel tells a different story. In *Meek as a Mustang*, Ryan Miller exposes that illusion and offers a far more compelling vision—one where true strength is not something we prove, but something we yield. This is a timely call back to the kind of power that defined the life of Jesus—and the kind that, if embraced, will not just reshape our lives, but radically reorder what we believe strength really is.

COLBY F. MAIER, founder of the Academy of the Bible

Meek as a Mustang is the book I've been waiting for someone to write. Ryan Miller doesn't ask you to shrink. He doesn't ask you to behave. He hands you a mirror and shows you that the fire you've been apologizing for your whole life is the very thing Jesus desires. Meekness isn't weakness; it's a wild heart that has finally found its leader. *Meek as a Mustang* recovers a word the church has fumbled for generations and gives meekness back the muscle Jesus put on it. Read this if you've ever been told your fire was the problem. It's not. It's just been waiting on the right master.

JACOB COYNE, founder of Stay Here, author of *The Secret Life of Christians*

Ryan Miller is a rare voice today. He is tender enough to reach the wounded and bold enough to tell the truth. In *Meek as a Mustang*, he takes a word the church has domesticated into passivity and restores it to its full, dangerous, biblical weight. In a cultural moment when cancel culture has replaced conviction and cutting people off has replaced reconciliation, Ryan's reframe is nothing short of prophetic. He recovers what the church has forgotten: Meekness is not the absence of strength; it is strength on its knees.

GRANT SKELDON, Next Gen Director for THINQ, author of *The Passion Generation*

RYAN MILLER
WITH KATIE M. KELLEY

MEEK AS A MUSTANG

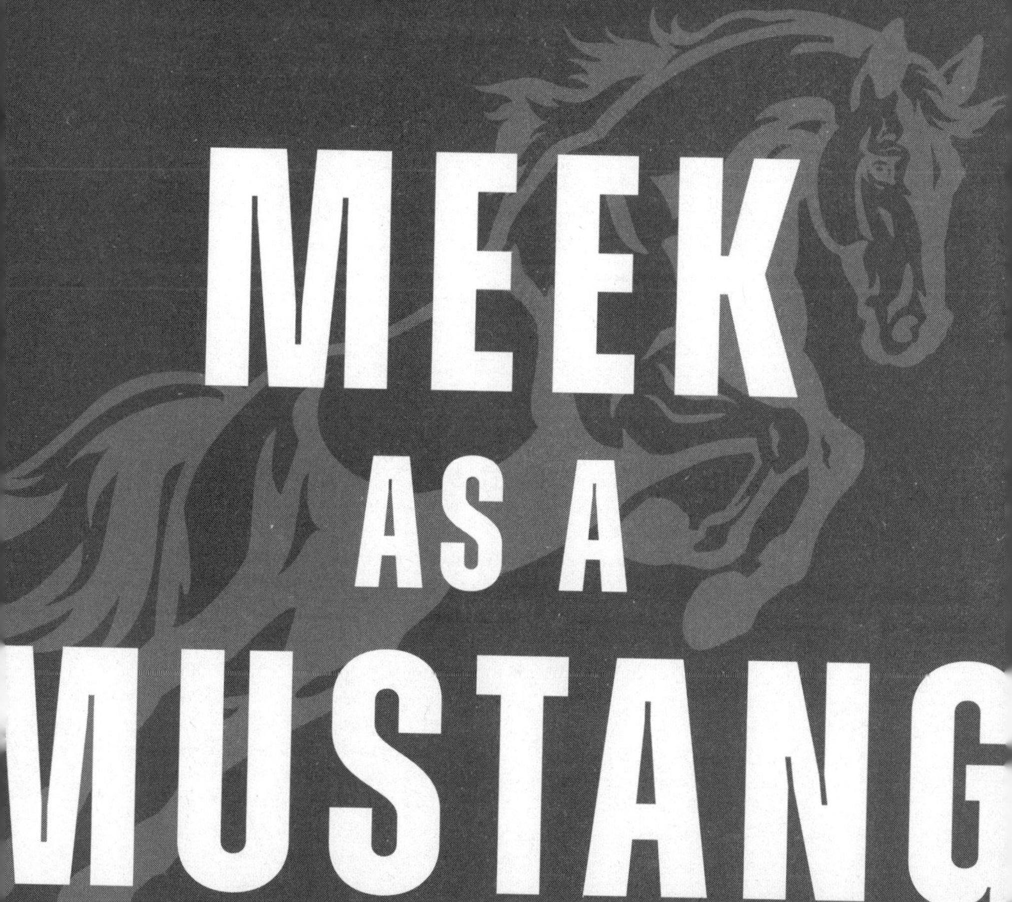

FIND THE STRENGTH TO SURRENDER YOUR WILD HEART TO JESUS

Visit Tyndale online at tyndale.com.

Visit the author online at thejesuspeoplemovement.com.

Meek as a Mustang: Find the Strength to Surrender Your Wild Heart to Jesus

Cover design by Dean H. Renninger

Interior design by Laura Cruise

Edited by Claire Lloyd

The author is represented by Alive Literary Agency, aliveliterary.com.

Library of Congress Cataloging-in-Publication Data
A catalog record for this book is available from the Library of Congress.

ISBN 979-8-4005-1716-7

Printed in the United States of America

32 31 30 29 28 27 26
7 6 5 4 3 2 1

This book is dedicated to my brothers and sisters whose hearts are desperate for the presence of God. Surrender the reins to him, and you will discover what it truly means to "inherit the earth."

CONTENTS

INTRODUCTION

"KNOCK IT OFF!!"

"HEY!! I said, '*Knock it off*,' guys!" Coach bellowed as he strode over to me with purpose. He called out to the assistant coach to take over practice, and I used the distraction to give my teammate one more shove in the chest.

"Miller! Dugout, *now*!" Coach directed me, pointing with an outstretched baseball bat for emphasis. His eyes were narrowed, his jaw set firm. I stormed toward the dugout, still roiling inside from the scuffle with the other boy over—I don't know, who got to shag fly balls next? Who could spit sunflower shells the farthest? Maybe it was a sarcastic comment about the fact that I *hadn't* actually made the baseball team and was just there for recreational practice—basically glorified PE class.

Coach marched after me, and when we reached the dugout, I whirled around with defiance plastered all over my face, ready for another fight. I so badly wanted to impress Coach because I so badly wanted to play ball. But right then, I was *hot*.

"He started it!" I shouted. "He—"

"I don't care *who* started it," he cut me off. "Ryan, this is unacceptable. This is the third fight I've had to break up, and *you*"—he pointed the bat square at my chest—"are at the center of every one. Out there"—he stretched out the bat toward the field—"you're part of a team, and I expect you to act like it."

I hate to admit it, but this was par for the course for me. Yep, I was *that* kid on the baseball diamond, and in life. Impulsive, a hothead, the prankster, one of the "wild ones" teachers were glad to pass through their classes just so they didn't have to deal with me anymore.

"You're all passion, Miller," Coach said, clearly exasperated, looking to the sky as if pleading for help. *Here it comes*, I thought. I knew I was a screwup. I knew Coach was one more person I had finally pushed too far. *Here comes the suspension, the call home. Banished from baseball for good, probably.* But Coach lowered his gaze and took a deep breath, calming both himself and the tension in the air. He put his hand on my shoulder, looked me in the eye, and said something that will stick with me for the rest of my life: "But Ryan, know this: I would rather tame a mustang than inspire a mule."

I'd rather tame a mustang . . .

Something about that comment stuck. It was the first time anyone had ever described my behavior in a positive light. Coach didn't want me to lose my fire; he wanted me to *use* it in the right way.

I couldn't stop thinking about it. And it changed everything.

After graduation, I became a youth pastor and focused my efforts on the kids most people saw as the outcasts. When they bucked and kicked, I told them the same thing Coach told me: "I'd rather tame a mustang than inspire a mule."

"Mustang" became a new identity for them, a badge of honor. They started to see their passion not as a liability but as a gift, and that made all the difference in the world.

Take Matt, for example. Matt was a good dude who had happened to get into a bit of trouble with the law, and he was trying to turn things around. I was living with a couple other guys, and we had room for one more, so I invited Matt to come live with us. At first, he wasn't so sure he wanted to move in with a bunch of Christians. But once he discovered that we all had a bit of a wild side—messing around, getting into trouble, and pranking people—he settled right into the group. And for the first time in his life, Matt didn't feel like an outsider. He had finally found his tribe.

After a few months of discipleship, Matt fell in love with Jesus. In fact, he was so on fire for God and his gospel of forgiveness and mercy, Matt decided to dedicate his life to telling other people about it and accepted a ministry position in Appalachia.

Matt never made it to his new job. He fell asleep at the wheel of his car while driving out there and hit a tree at seventy miles per hour. He died instantly.

I was devastated. In my mind, Matt was the consummate mustang—fiery and passionate. Rough around the edges. Wild and untamed. The complete opposite of what most people think of when they hear the word *Christian*. And yet he was completely sold out for the Lord. I couldn't wait to see how God would use a testimony like his.

I struggled in the wake of Matt's death for months. I

couldn't make sense of his loss. I couldn't see the meaning of it. I had to make a change in my life to try to regain some sense of control. I quit my ministry position and dedicated my life to finding some way of honoring Matt. And the best way I could think to do that was to show the world how much God loves and wants to use the wild ones—the mustangs.

This is a book about my failure—and God's success—in that pursuit. I have had the blessing of knowing many of God's "mustangs" in my life, and I'm honored to share some of their stories in this book. And if there's one thing he's taught me along the way, it's that the single greatest marker of world-changing, table-turning, disruptive wild ones for his Kingdom is *meekness*.

That's right. Meekness. As in, "Blessed are the meek . . ."[1]

It's striking to realize that the one time Jesus described what he is like to his disciples in his own words, he said this: "I am meek and lowly in heart."[2] Not forgiving, not loving, not righteous, wise, holy, sacrificial, or any of the other wonderful ways we know his character.

"I am meek," he said. "Learn from me."

Throughout this book, you'll be challenged to learn from Jesus—to pause, reflect, and act boldly in "Meek Moments" that will draw you closer to him. But meekness is not what you think. The prevailing cultural understanding sees meekness as timid, shy, a quiet disposition, someone who would never "rock the boat." But let's hold that understanding of meekness up to Jesus: Meek and lowly Jesus fasted for forty days in the desert and withstood direct attacks from Satan, wielding Scripture as his sword.[3] Meek Jesus brandished a whip and flipped tables in the Temple.[4] He is the same Jesus who stood silent before his accusers, able to call down legions of angels, and yet went boldly to the cross.[5] And you won't find one circumstance where Jesus was afraid to "rock the boat."

Meekness is not a personality trait. It's a character virtue. It is the radically countercultural strength to live with your eyes so fixed on your master, Jesus, that your heart and mind want his desires, not yours.

God used a simple but profound encouragement from my coach to reach me, a wild mustang of a boy, and to validate the fire that he put inside of me. Then, God drew me to himself in seasons of profound loss and began reaching the hardest parts of my heart. He began teaching me about what it truly means to be meek, like him.

And he used mustangs—real thousand-pound, hooves-flying, nostrils-flaring, wild mustangs—to do it.

As I set out to make some meaning of Matt's death—really, of his *life*—I started looking into this idea of taming mustangs. As usual, much like that day on the baseball field, I really didn't have a plan. I was charging forward, full of passion, with no idea what I was doing and absolutely no clue how much God would change my life in the process.

That's when I met Grant.

CHAPTER 1

IT'S YOUR RELATIONSHIP

One thing have I asked of the LORD, that I will seek after: that I may dwell in the house of the LORD all the days of my life, to gaze upon the beauty of the LORD and to inquire in his temple.

PSALM 27:4, ESV

We do not know what to do, but our eyes are on you.

2 CHRONICLES 20:12, ESV

I met Grant about ten years ago, as I was researching and reading everything I could find about horses. I had the idea to create a rehabilitation program that could change wild lives—while actually taming wild mustangs. In a reaction to my own angst, I wanted to show that those whom the world—and to be honest, Christianity—had written off as "too much" or "too far gone" could actually become the most bold and fearless men and women of God.

I dove into researching wild mustangs, learning everything I could and reaching out to horse trainers all over the country, telling them about my idea and asking for help—even when they had absolutely no idea who I was. I sent hundreds of emails, relentless in my efforts to get this project off the ground. After Grant, a world-renowned mustang trainer, received my email about the idea I had to start the rehabilitation program, he called me and, through a shaky voice, said, "That's my story. I'd love to be part of this." He invited me to his ranch in Oklahoma, where he would show me firsthand what it was like to be in a round pen with a mustang.

Grant is the doppelgänger of Woody from *Toy Story*, with a hardened edge like the Marlboro Man, a connoisseur of one-liners. As we walked up to the round pens on his property, Grant hummed a country song with a slight grin on his face. I hadn't a clue what I was getting myself into.

"I can already feel it," said Grant in a soft but sure voice. "It's like stepping into a sacred space with something wild and unpredictable."

I would learn eventually that Grant said things like this all the time—phrases that made whoever was listening stop and wonder what he really meant. But at the time, I didn't know what he was talking about. From the stories he had been sharing and the countenance on his face, I got the sense that he thought this was about to be a profound spiritual experience for me. I wasn't quite buying it—what he said seemed a little hippieish, especially coming from a cowboy. I understood the weight of what we were doing, of course. A wild mustang can weigh up to one thousand pounds, and at any second it could stomp the yard on me. I had read about how many trainers have been badly injured or even killed by horses, most with a swift kick to the dome. I wasn't overly concerned, though, until we made our way to the outer edge of the metal pen where a mustang paced. My heart started racing as I got up close. The horse looked much bigger than he did from the truck.

"This here is Amarillo," Grant said, pointing to the massive sandy-coated hunk of muscle nervously huffing and stomping back and forth in the pen. "What do you want to do with him?"

Uhh, I don't know, man—you're the mustang trainer, I thought to myself. I couldn't take my eyes off this beautiful, golden, wild mustang, heavily breathing what looked like plumes of smoke in the cold Oklahoma morning. I was silent, so Grant asked again, "What do you want to do with him?"

"I have no idea," I said with a nervous laugh. "Is he safe?"

"Of course *he* isn't safe. He's a wild mustang! But don't worry. I won't let you get hurt."

I saw my buddy standing outside the pen with his camera filming, since we were thinking of making a movie docu menting the program and time on the ranch, and I had the thought, *If I make this horse get real wild in the pen, we could get some good footage out of it.* So that's what I decided to do. "I think I want to make him go crazy!" I told Grant.

"Well, go out there and make him go crazy, then."

"Is that okay?" I asked.

"It's your relationship," Grant responded.

I jumped down from the side of the pen and confidently

walked into the ring. As I started making my way toward the mustang, adrenaline mixed with fear washed through my body. Amarillo pawed his foot aggressively into the ground, like a bull with a matador in front of him.

"He's not gonna kill me, is he?" I asked in my steadiest sounding voice.

"I won't let you get hurt," Grant said again, with that slight grin on his face, still making me feel like I was going to make a fool of myself.

I took two more cautious steps toward the horse and had a sudden awareness of fear, and it wasn't just mine. I could feel the horse's fear too. We were in a standoff, staring at each other, wondering who was going to make the first move. Amarillo held his ground as I inched closer. But then a slight twitch in his massive shoulder sent a jerk through my nervous system. "Grant?" I said in a low voice, not taking my eyes off the horse.

"Yes, Ryan?" he called back.

"I'm not sure what to do . . ."

"It depends on what you want to do. It's your relationship," Grant repeated.

Stop saying that, I thought. *Some actual directions would be nice.*

As the mustang angled his head toward me, I knew he was anxious. He paced back and forth, not so much as giving a look my way but making it clear that he knew I was there. It was obvious this horse wanted nothing to do with me. And that was a challenge.

"I'm gonna touch him," I said, unable to hide the nervous excitement in my voice.

"Well, then, go right on up there and touch him," Grant said.

I edged closer and closer. Just as I was about to make my move, the mustang lunged forward, cut hard to the right, darted, and hurled his body away from me. Trapped in this pen, Amarillo thrashed and bucked all of his weight in aggressive thrusts, nearly paralyzing me with fear. But I rallied my resolve and started chasing him in a chaotic game of tag in the arena.

My quest to touch Amarillo went on for a few minutes as we both got more and more tired, with neither of us giving up. I refused to let him win, and in his mind, he probably thought I was a predator, so he continued to cut and dart away from me. We were both caught up in the whirl of dust, and our lungs and legs were both fading.

Out of sheer exhaustion, Amarillo made a move toward the edge of the arena. It's almost as if he'd had enough of my taunting and wanted to escape. He was so tired that he crashed into the side, causing the fence to sway against his weight. It cracked and split just enough to cut the mustang's leg. The sound of the crash, coupled with a heavy exhale of pain and the sight of blood dripping from the horse's leg, stunned me. I knew I had gone too far, and I scrambled back toward Grant. The mustang pulled up and maneuvered away from me.

"Whoa, whoa, whoa!" Grant shouted, already hopping down from the rail.

I was shocked. I couldn't believe what I had done. I sheepishly walked to the far side of the pen, praying Amarillo wasn't hurt too badly.

As the mustang regrouped in the space of my retreat, I watched him limp away, and I felt terrible. I fully recognized that this horse had blood dripping down its leg because of me and my lack of patience to do things his way. I closed my eyes and allowed the moment to take hold, standing out of the way while Grant tried to get close enough to Amarillo to see the wound. The blood made the cut look worse than it was, and it would heal up before long, but that didn't matter. I was still the reason this horse was hurt, and it was completely unnecessary.

Grant pulled me aside. There were a few moments of silence as I hung my head and Grant stood next to me with his hand on my shoulder. "You know, man, you walked into this pen with an agenda. It started even before you set foot in here. It was a mindset. A goal. A desire to get your needs met before meeting the needs of the horse. You were gonna touch that horse. Show him who was boss. Like every other predator he's been running from his entire life. And look at him now, more convinced that you are a predator than when you walked in." I glanced across the pen at Amarillo as I took in Grant's words, evidence of my recklessness still fresh on the horse's leg, and nodded.

"This horse picks up on things and feels them more deeply than you and I ever could because he's spent his life running from threats like you. It's why for years, trainers have done nothing but break mustangs, not tame them. They'll rope them, wrestle them to the ground, and sit on their heads to demoralize them. And the sad part is, it works. Kind of. That horse will become broken. He will comply, but he will never be loyal, because that wild, bold spirit inside of him breaks too. It takes a loving trainer who wants to build a real relationship to truly tame a mustang. Once that relationship is safe enough and that horse can look at you and no longer see a predator, taming that wildness becomes worth something. The problem is, it's a rare person who wants to take the time to get the mustang to realize that the trainer is not a predator, that he's there to gentle this horse so they can accomplish something together."

He stopped and looked at me as tears filled his eyes. I started to get it. Grant was not just talking about wild mustangs.

MEEK MOMENT

God will not force us to obey him. We can stomp and kick and buck, thinking we are really doing a lot in this world, unaware that our hustle to be somebody is focused on things with no eternal value. After a while, nobody is impressed by a wild mustang running around a pen. Nobody "oohs" and "aahs" at the amount of dust we can kick up or the dents we can create.

What is impressive is when a mustang becomes a warhorse, running fearlessly into battle. A true, loyal warhorse is formed not by hustle and punishment but by respect and patience. It has the humility to continually align its love with the loving gaze of its master.

To embrace meekness, we have to stop and see a God who is patiently waiting for us to receive his love—the perfect love displayed for us in Jesus' death on the cross. And when we do, we begin to trust his character and his promises. It's when we trust him with our whole lives that he can take us outside the pen for a journey that is more than we could ask or imagine.[1]

After my talk with Grant, I took a beat for a minute and found a seat on the tailgate of his truck, gazing off into the distance. I occasionally glanced at the round pen to see Amarillo staring back at me, blood now drying on his pale coat. I wanted to walk over and tell him how sorry I was, but I stopped myself and turned to look off into the sunset over the flat Oklahoma horizon.

Grant eventually found me again and hopped up on the tailgate, clearly recognizing the processing going on in my mind. "Wanna know how you tame a mustang?" he asked.

"Yeah," I told him, lifting my head a bit.

"Well, it begins with love. These horses will tell you quite a lot about yourself, and this horse just told you some things, didn't he?" Grant said, leaning in with a grin.

I gave a slight exhale and chuckle, my posture humble.

"It all starts with a look. That's it. That's really all there is to it," Grant added. I looked at him, a bit confused.

"If that horse can stop running like mad around that pen for just a second to look at you, and if the only thing on your mind is loving that horse and giving him what he needs first, before meeting your own needs, well, you've tamed your mustang."

He let his words sit with me for a second. Then he went on.

"It's all about acknowledgment. When you walk into that round pen, you apply pressure by walking toward the horse, getting it to move around. Sooner or later, it's gonna get a little curious and turn its head and look at you. At that moment, you back off and give the horse the space it needs. As you pursue that mustang over and over and allow him to acknowledge—every time he looks at you—that you are there for his benefit, he's gonna start to follow you. Eventually, he's gonna trust you enough to let you touch him. And when he receives that touch, he's gonna heal." Grant paused for a moment, then added with a slight break in his voice, "And you're gonna heal in ways you could never imagine. But it starts with a look. And then, the one thing this mustang was scared of most will change his world."

RADICAL LOVE

That day, Grant showed the gospel to me in a way I had never experienced. It was deeper than words. And it made me think about all the relational round pens I had walked into in my life. I saw a picture of how I had treated people around me—pursuing my own agenda in ministry, daily life, and even in my marriage. I began to understand in a new way how God pursues wild people and how wild people can choose meekness. It's his kindness that leads to repentance, not forcing us into a corner to shame us into better behavior.[2] The image of God's patient, loving gaze on me felt like a drink of cold water on a hot day.

I could see my sin and the grace and love of God at the same time.

God is after us. Not to harm us, force us into submission, or get something from us—but to love us into relationship with him. Followers of Jesus are motivated to live out of the freedom of that love, not the fear of punishment. Jesus will continue pursuing us even if we run, buck, and kick away from him. But intimacy with the one we were created to live for begins when we stop, even just for a second, to truly acknowledge who he is.

MEEK MOMENT

Close your eyes to envision what God's face looks like when he gazes at you. What do you see? If you see a judge with his finger pointed, or anyone other than a loving Father, you might still be running around the pen. God wants us to know he has no agenda other than transforming our hearts through his love. Becoming meek doesn't mean changing your nature—it's turning your gaze toward the God who cares for you.

I understand this more now as a father. I want to do everything I can to let my son know that I want the world for him. I want him to experience a glimpse of my love, even if that means making silly faces and acting a fool to get him to smile. I'll do anything to pass my joy to him, but he has to see it in my face.

Psalm 67:1 says, "May God be gracious to us and bless us and make his face shine on us." The line "make his face shine on us" can be pictured as a father doing everything he can to get his baby to smile.[3] It's a prayer that the hearer would truly know the presence of a loving father. This goofy, fun-loving nature may not be how you see God. The idea of God as a dad being silly with a baby is so far from how we often think about God that it is easy to miss out on this mind-blowing understanding of his true opinion of us. He loves us! He wants joy for us. And he wants to take us on an adventure with him outside the pen.

The day after my encounter with Amarillo, we went back to the round pen, and Grant walked me through the steps of getting acknowledgment from the mustang. Grant had me start to walk toward the horse. Taking just two steps made Amarillo panic and run like crazy around the pen. But no matter how skittish this horse was, I was instructed by Grant to continue pursuing and to wait for the mustang to slightly turn his head to look at me.

I made a few attempts at getting this look from Amarillo, but acknowledgment was slow going. Finally, as I was walking to the other side of the pen with my back to the horse, I heard Grant shout to look at what Amarillo was doing. I carefully turned my head, and there he was.

"No way!" I shouted, giddy with excitement yet trying to play it cool, to not lose this thread of trust we had built. This same wild mustang I had traumatized the day before, the one who had thrashed and kicked and tried desperately to get as far away from me as possible, was slowly yet confidently following me around the pen.

"You see, Ryan, when this horse begins to acknowledge your goodness, he'll start to follow you. And once he's made that decision to follow, you have the honor of giving him the very thing he's longed for his whole life yet didn't know how to get: a relationship. You've taken this horse that's been passed over for years for being 'too far gone' and made him a partner."

Tears welled up in my eyes. I was *experiencing* the gospel, and it was healing something in me that I didn't even realize I longed for. As that horse began to see my heart for him, I began to see God's heart for me.

Something changes in your soul when someone acknowledges you even though you don't think you are worthy of acknowledgment. The idea that God would come for the most gnarly and mangled among us is incredible, but it's true. God wants the throwaways, the people branded with condemnation for all to see, those who stubbornly keep running from the one who just wants a turn of the head.

The apostle Peter makes the shocking statement that

God has adopted us into his family and made us into a royal priesthood—taking us from rags to riches, orphan to son or daughter, wild mustang to warhorse in the King's army.[4] Only when we acknowledge this radical love can the wild and reckless nature inside of us be crafted into an instrument in the hands of a master. This is the beginning of meekness: an acknowledgment of God's goodness that leads us to surrender to an ultimate, loving authority. A perfect, trustworthy one.

If you're like me, you may have experienced a church leader, pastor, or Christian who focused more on rules than on Jesus. You may think of God as being more concerned with behavior modification than heart transformation through love. It happens so often: Leaders, not knowing how to reconcile wildness with some of the unspoken rules of tidied-up church culture, try to move people toward a safe, streamlined version of following Jesus. As Christians, we are often more comfortable with rules and checked boxes, like perfect church attendance and generous tithing, than someone so in love with Jesus that they would do anything for him or go anywhere he asked.

But over the years, this is what God has taught me: Meekness can look like bold obedience to the Lord. As someone who has felt judged for the majority of my life, it's healing to realize that Jesus wants me and can use me for his purposes, in the middle of my wildness.

It's human nature to want to change something that looks wild. The Pharisees saw Jesus' ministry and were so offended by how radically outside the parameters of traditional Judaism he went to win hearts that they could think of nothing other than stopping his work, stopping the man they saw as too wild.[5]

This tendency is in all of us. It was certainly my posture toward Amarillo. With the knowledge of God's perfection, and with our deep understanding of the untamed parts of our souls, it seems to make sense that we would need to fix the wildness in us before a perfect God could see value in us. But our shortcomings are never the disqualifiers. In God's economy, our weakness is made perfect in his strength.[6] God never uses a humiliating training tactic when he tames you into who he made you to be. Instead, he draws you to him with the patient look of a loving trainer, inviting you into the safest relationship you'll ever know.

So what will you do? There is a world of adventure out there, battles to fight alongside a loving God who gives us hope and a future for eternity. But it begins with a look. Do you see it?

It's your relationship.

CHAPTER 2

WHY WOULD YOU WANT A MUSTANG?

"My son," the father said, "you are always with me, and everything I have is yours. But we had to celebrate and be glad, because this brother of yours was dead and is alive again; he was lost and is found."

LUKE 15:31-32

From a young age, I was a bit of a paradox. I loved Jesus but spent most of my time with the crew that others would have classified as "the bad kids." I brought my friends to church as often as they would allow, usually with the promise of a sleepover and pranking antics the night before. On one particular Sunday morning when I dragged my buddies to church, I could tell from their nervous laughter that they didn't really know what to do or how to act as we walked in the building. We made it through the lobby and into the back room where the youth group was meeting, and we might as well have walked in without clothes on, the way the room quieted as a few dozen kids stopped talking and stared at us. Some girls approached our group and, snickering under their breath, asked, "What are *you guys* doing here?" Would it surprise you that those friends of mine never did come back to church with me?

As Christians, we seem to be attracted to the type of person that plays it safe—the buttoned-up rule follower, the "fall in line" order taker, the honor roll students and seminary graduates. We get nervous about the wild ones—the people who like to take risks or shake things up, the ones who ask the hard questions, who have a colorful past. These kinds of people walk into a church, and based on their reputation or what they look like, other people turn their heads to say, "What are *they* doing here?"

But this group—the wild ones—often includes the best kind of leaders. The kind of leaders the church desperately needs.

My generation, and the generation after, are exiting the American church in massive numbers. Research shows that over one million young people are running from the church and from the Christian faith every year. If this trend continues, by the year 2034, less than a decade from the time of this writing, over ten million young people who grew up in our church communities will have left their faith, leaving the buildings—and more important, the hearts of so many people—empty.[1] There are many reasons someone might leave the church, but I have to wonder—have we somehow created an environment for young Christians that is focused so heavily on respectable behavior that we've made church a place you can attend only if you fit the mold? What if the church, a place that is supposed to be a hospital for the broken, has now become so sanitized that it rejects the people Jesus spent his entire ministry calling to follow him?

The church today might be keeping the mustang-spirited people at a distance, but what we see in Scripture is a different picture. It was the wild ones that Jesus called to pick up their cross and follow him.[2]

Why do we run from what feels messy when the idea of "taming the wild" captures the entire narrative of how God rescues his people over and over again? The Bible is the story of a rebellious people pursued by a gracious and loving God. We play it far too safe, and we have gotten far too comfortable. Taming mustangs is risky work. After all, a wild mustang can kill you if threatened. So instead, we cage the bold and shut down their potential, and we get back to our ice cream socials. In our culture today, the word *meek* is associated more often with a mouse than a warhorse. And the church has been pursuing mice when all along we should have been roping mustangs.

MEEK MOMENT

Nobody is too wild for God. The late Timothy Keller described the gospel like this: "We are more sinful and flawed in ourselves than we ever dared believe, yet at the very same time we are more loved and accepted in Jesus Christ than we ever dared hope."[3] How can this be? How could someone so big, so good, so holy and perfect as God look at us and see *everything*—our motives, our secret thoughts, our sneaky tendencies, perhaps a shameful past—and still treasure us as he would his own child? The answer is simple: because he looks at us and he *does* see his Son and because the punishment we deserve was already placed on Jesus on the cross.

My desire for the program on the ranch was to show the virtue underneath the bucking and "bad behavior" of untamed lives. I wanted people to see that the Kingdom of God is meant to take this wildness and tame it into something valuable and usable. After all, God took Moses, a murderer, and elevated him to a position of leadership over the Israelites. He took David, a shepherd boy turned king with a record of murder and adultery, and tamed him into a man after his own heart, bringing the Messiah from his family line. Then Jesus rounded up a group of ragtag teenage fishermen, a revolutionary, and a tax collector. Simon Peter couldn't get his foot out of his mouth, and a couple of brothers were so volatile that Jesus nicknamed them the Sons of Thunder.[4] He tamed these men with the heart of a loving teacher and sent them to the ends of the earth to spread the gospel, to suffer for a cause only mustangs would be loyal enough to die for.

That's why I wanted to find bold young men like the ones Jesus chose, exceptional leaders, bucking with wild but filled with potential. Three untamed mustangs using their wild for the wrong purposes and in all the wrong places. We had all the logistics in place for the program; we just had to find our mustangs.

Our search started by reaching out to personal contacts in ministry as well as various parachurch organizations, but we weren't finding anyone who felt like the best fit for the program. So I went back to the young men I knew, the ones I had been discipling for years as a youth pastor, and I asked them about their own peers: "Who is the best leader you know; who is just misguided?" It wasn't hard at all for these young men to identify the people who fit that description. We started making calls, interviewing, and asking the Lord for discernment.

Within a few months, we had chosen three boys I was confident were perfect for this experience. The first was Landon, an eighteen-year-old from San Antonio who had already been to jail several times. He'd spent over a year at a group home for troubled boys and was also a prominent drug dealer in his area. Landon, or "Dingo" as his friends called him, showed up to our FaceTime call so high on drugs that he couldn't even answer the questions clearly. After our interview, we got a text from Landon's friend, the one who had set him up with this opportunity to go to the ranch. He told us how much Landon was kicking himself for the state he'd shown up in for the interview, thinking he had blown his chance. But that's not what was going through my mind. This young man showed up for a chance at redemption even in the midst of his addiction? *This is exactly who I want*, I thought. Landon was definitely a mustang.

The next two young men we chose were Caleb, who'd grown up being woken by gunfire and known childhood trauma from an early age, and Dawson, who'd endured severe child abuse and homelessness, leading to gang life, drug abuse, and jail time. The more I talked to them, the more confident I was that we had our three mustangs.

At this point, things should have felt complete. We had three participants who were quintessential mustangs, and I had full confidence that they could not only put on an impressive show but that they had passion that could change the world if they were able to channel their reckless, wild spirits. But something felt off in my spirit that I couldn't quite nail down. In the moment when I should have been celebrating our three young men being chosen, I had this gnawing feeling that someone else was out there. It was like the Holy Spirit kept tapping my shoulder to keep looking, even with less than a month until we were supposed to start the program.

The more I thought and prayed about it, the more sure I became about continuing our search. So we scrambled, scouring every resource, but we had no leads. I started to wonder if I had dragged us down a dead end.

Then one of our team members, Kelsey, called. "I think I found our last mustang, Ryan. I didn't even think twice about him as an option before, because he is still in prison. But he has a court case happening in three days. We have to go!"

Right away, I looked up this young man on Facebook, and my eyes grew wide at what I saw. Lucas had tattoos from head to toe, a gold grill in his mouth, a profile page filled with posts about women and money, and photos and videos of himself clearly intoxicated, incoherently rapping about dealing drugs while throwing money. Everything Kelsey had told me about Lucas didn't seem to fit what I was seeing. "So you're telling me he's a really sweet guy, great leader and all, but he just has a history of violence, was gang affiliated, and made a living as a drug dealer?" It was clear that Lucas could be the kind of living contradiction that we were looking for, but I'll admit, I was nervous. I told Kelsey I wanted to talk with him.

That night I called Lucas in jail. I could barely make out what he was saying with the combination of his deep voice and the poor quality of the prison phone. In a broken tone, Lucas kept repeating over and over, "I just want to make something of my life." That sentiment I heard loud and clear.

As we talked, my judgments toward Lucas began to break, as did my heart. But Lucas was up for a twelve-year sentence, and getting him out of that sentence for a chance to come to the ranch was a long shot. A real long shot.

Kelsey and I both felt strongly that Lucas was our guy. Even though it seemed like an impossible mission, he was worth the chance. We started thinking of all we could do to pull off this Hail Mary. We made brochures to show the judge that this was a credible rehabilitation program. We rallied everyone we could to start praying for a miracle.

I called my mentor, Riley, a former Navy SEAL. I had met Riley a few years before, when some mutual ministry friends knew that I was thinking about trying to be a Navy SEAL as well. Riley quickly became a trusted friend and confidant to me, because he knew what it meant to have Jesus change your life and then to overcome circumstances most of us would call unthinkable. Riley's childhood was like Lucas's in many ways. He was once a drug dealer in the Bronx, and he'd had his share of run-ins with the law. When I told him about Lucas, Riley was silent. Then he said, "You do know that I was on my way to jail when a Navy recruiter came to my court case and advocated for me? I'll be there."

That Friday, we gathered in the parking lot of the courthouse and prayed for a miracle. I was as nervous as I can ever remember being in my life. We walked through the metal detectors and up the stairs to the dark courtroom. I squeezed my wife Annie's hand, and I know she could feel how sweaty my palms were as we waited for the judge to walk out and sit on his judgment seat, which towered above everyone. Finally, the bailiff called, "All rise!" and we waited, as boy after boy was escorted across the room with their hands and feet shackled, about to have the next years of their lives determined by this judge.

After about an hour, the judge called for Lucas. He walked into the courtroom, and right away, it was clear that there was something different about him, just from his appearance. He was striking and carried a strong presence about him, but there was humility in the way he walked into the room. Lucas first looked at the judge above him, but knowing we were there, he started to turn his head to look back at the audience. The bailiff quickly grabbed him by the shoulders and snapped him around, shouting, "Look forward!"

The proceeding began, and Lucas's public defender made his case to the judge. He frequently was cut off by the district attorney, who clearly had the upper hand in this case. With the palpable sense that this case was slipping away from him, the public defender said, "Your honor, Lucas has been accepted into a rehabilitation program, and I would like Ryan Miller, the director of that program, along with some of his associates, to come up and speak."

I froze. I had been given no prior warning that I would have to speak. I'd expected that maybe I would stand up, smile, wave, point to the brochures, and call it a day. But there I was, stomach in knots as I made my way toward the front of the courtroom to speak in front of the judge. I didn't have enough time to full-on panic, but I was close.

I broke into my impromptu speech about the work we would be doing at the ranch, how Lucas would be participating in equine-assisted psychotherapy, and how taming and training wild mustangs would give these young men a picture of themselves. I continued my pitch with "Your Honor, they say, 'Tame the mustang, you tame the man . . . '" but then the judge cut me off.

"Why do you want *him*?" he asked, pulling his glasses down and leaning forward with undisguised curiosity.

"Well, Your Honor, I believe that sometimes the best leaders are just a little misguided."

"A little misguided?" he asked, chuckling while he aggressively shuffled through his papers and began to read the long list of all Lucas's offenses from the time he was sixteen years old. "Let me get this right: You want me to allow a convicted felon off of a twelve-year sentence to go play with some horses?"

I thought his question was a rhetorical slap to the face, but he continued, "I want an answer!"

"Yes, Your Honor," I replied as I shrank a few inches.

"Well, young man, even if I wanted to let this happen, it would need to go through the district attorney. You mean to tell me that you believe the district attorney is going to look the other way? You do realize what you are asking for?"

I responded as confidently as my wounded ego would allow and said, "Yes, Your Honor, I know what I'm asking for."

"Well, okay then," he said as he sat back in his chair and motioned for me to leave. The public defender then called up Riley, who was next in line.

Riley began, in a voice broken by the emotions he was holding back, "Your Honor, I was just like this young man, standing before a judge, guilty. But someone saw something in me and came to my defense when I didn't deserve it. They gave me a chance for a new life. So that's why I'm here now, asking for the same thing for Lucas." He walked away, and you could hear a pin drop in the room. I had never seen Riley get the slightest bit emotional before, and here he was in tears over someone whose life was so much like his once was.

As I was standing off to the side in the front of the courtroom, doing my best to emotionally keep it together, I looked back to see that the entire audience had filled up with spectators. Word had spread throughout the courthouse that something out of the ordinary was happening, so a small crowd had gathered to watch.

The judge sat back in his chair, obviously shocked by the level of support Lucas was getting from people who'd come from all over the country to stand by him in his defense.

The last person to speak on Lucas's behalf was his childhood friend. He made his way to the front of the courtroom to advocate for his buddy. This friend was no angel himself, having been arrested twenty-three times and having recently stood before this very judge. Still, he sheepishly walked up to Lucas's side and, with his head hanging low, said, "Your Honor, I know I'm in no position to be speaking to you right now."

The judge replied, "Actually, you're in just as good of a position as anyone, so please proceed."

"Your Honor, I know Lucas has done a lot of bad things, and I know people see him as a really bad guy, but he is the best leader I know. When we were younger, whenever someone was getting picked on, Lucas was the one coming to their defense. So I'm asking you, Your Honor, to see the Lucas that I know and not the Lucas that the rest of the world sees."

As Lucas's friend made his way back to our group, the judge sat there in thought. Lucas's grandma was in the back row, and we could hear her loudly praying, "Lord Jesus, move in this courtroom. Move in this courtroom, Lord!"

The judge stared off into the distance before speaking up.

"I don't know what to do!" he said, burdened. "This opportunity sounds great, but what you guys are asking me to do is impossible. You want me to look past a twelve-year sentence in favor of a rehabilitation program? The only thing I can do is delay the hearing."

My heart dropped. There was nothing we could do. I was deflated and embarrassed. We had filled Lucas's family with hope that we might be able to get him out of his twelve-year sentence, and we had failed. Our group gathered outside the courtroom, not knowing what to say to one another. Lucas's grandma gave me a hug, thankful for the effort we had made, but everyone was aware that we did not get the answer we wanted.

All of a sudden, the doors swung open, and the district attorney came storming out. She marched right up to me, pointed her finger in my face, and asked, "Why are you doing this?"

I was taken aback, but I gathered my thoughts and said, "Well, ma'am, it's the gospel. Jesus left ninety-nine sheep to go after the lost one, and right now, Lucas is the lost one."

She looked at me for a few seconds with a confused stare. And then, to my surprise, tears welled up in her eyes, and she began to cry. Lucas's grandma walked over and wrapped her up in her arms, saying, "Come here, sweetheart." They stood there embracing each other in tears outside the courtroom. After a few moments, the DA wiped her eyes and turned to me and Kelsey. "Come by my office on Monday, and let's see what we can do to make this happen."

That next week, the district attorney visited the judge and dropped the charges. Instead of serving a sentence of twelve years in prison, Lucas came to the ranch to heal from his wounds, be mentored, and tame a wild mustang.

The arc of Lucas's life story is longer than this chapter, and God is not done writing it. One night during that first week on the ranch, everyone was hanging out on the porch of the cabin telling jokes. In the middle of the fun, Lucas pulled me off to the side and asked if we could talk. As we walked down the dirt road, he stopped and faced me, then asked, "Ryan, why did you choose me?"

THE WILD ONES

In Scripture, the Pharisees asked a similar question. They saw Jesus in the company of people that the Pharisees themselves would never associate with, and they asked his disciples, "'Why does your teacher eat with tax collectors and sinners?' On hearing this, Jesus said, 'It is not the healthy who need a doctor, but the sick.'"[5]

In another Gospel account of Jesus eating dinner with the outcasts, Luke writes, "Now the tax collectors and sinners were all gathering around to hear Jesus. But the Pharisees and the teachers of the law muttered, 'This man welcomes sinners and eats with them.'"[6]

There were a few different people present here. First, the tax collectors and prostitutes, who were viewed as the scum of the earth and might as well have been metaphorically branded and thrown into holding facilities. Then there were the Pharisees and scribes—the religious elite of the day—who had been handpicked for their piety and intellect, men who were well-trained at finger-pointing. And then there was Jesus, who was a category unto himself, a man who claimed to be a holy rabbi yet was spending his time with the kind of people who would make his reputation questionable.

The Pharisees, seeing Jesus hanging out with the worst of the worst in society, huddled together, talking smack about him. "Look at this guy! He claims to be a prophet and the Son of God, yet he welcomes these low lives and even eats with them!"

To a first-century Jew, it was shameful to associate with someone considered to be a sinner, and to eat with them was next-level. But Jesus took the opportunity to turn around the religious leaders' slanderous comment and show his heart for the misfit mustang.

You see, when these Pharisees said, "This man welcomes sinners and eats with them," they thought they were putting Jesus on blast, but in reality, they were preaching the welcoming gospel message that Jesus had come to deliver to these mustang-spirited men and women: "This man welcomes sinners."

Scripture says, "This man *prosdechetai* sinners and eats with them." The word *prosdechomai* in the original New Testament Greek is for a deep, meaningful welcome.[7] This type of welcome is more intimate than we have a proper word for in English. This *prosdechomai* welcome is like a scene in a movie where a soldier arrives home from his tour of duty, walks off the plane, and greets his wife and kids as they run into his arms, tears of joy streaming down their faces. *Prosdechomai* is to say, "I see everything that you are and love everything you are."

So when Jesus hears the Pharisees' accusation, he tells them three stories that unpack the depth of his desire to lovingly *prosdechetai* these outcasts.

First, Jesus tells the story of a shepherd who had one hundred sheep. One dumb sheep runs away, and the shepherd leaves the ninety-nine sheep in the open country and goes after that one rebellious sheep.[8] This story gets told quite a bit in churches today—or outside a courtroom, in my case—and it seems like everyone finds it so beautiful that the shepherd leaves the ninety-nine to go after the wild one. But when I first heard the parable, it seemed irresponsible. It's beautiful that the shepherd goes after the wild one. But why would he risk so much? Why try to save just one?

Jesus, likely perceiving their confusion, breaks into his second story. There was a woman who had ten coins. She loses one coin and goes frantic, looking all over the house for it. When she finally finds the coin, she calls her friends over to celebrate with a party.[9] A party! The Pharisees probably had no clue what Jesus was talking about. A lady loses a coin, finds it, and throws a party. How is that even logical?

He tells them a third and final story. A son goes up to his dad and says, "I'm leaving, Dad. I want your money. I don't want you; give me my inheritance now." The dad, heartbroken but still allowing his son the freedom to choose to stay or go, gives his son the money. The son then runs off to a distant land—let's just call it Las Vegas—and parties his money away. And once he squanders all his dad's money on wild living, he ends up in a pigsty. In his humiliation, the son comes to his senses and reasons, "How many of my father's hired servants have food to spare, and here I am starving to death!"[10] So he makes a plan to return to his father, apologize for his sins, and ask to be a servant in his father's house. But when he returns, the father sees him from a long way off, girds up his tunic, and runs after his son.[11]

At this point in the story, both the Pharisees and sinners probably would have given an audible gasp, because for a Jewish man to bare his legs and run was one of the most shameful things he could do.[12] You may know this story as the parable of the prodigal son.

When the son saw his dad running toward him, he might have thought his dad was about to take him out with a nasty right hook to teach him a lesson. But instead, the father puts shoes on his son's feet, a cloak around his shoulders, and a ring on his finger, all to tell him that he is *welcome* back into the family. Lavish, undeserved, shocking *prosdechomai* love for the wildest mustang.

MEEK MOMENT

To believe that nothing can separate us from the love of Christ and then to become embodied agents of that love is the ultimate pursuit of our lives. There is no more important work for us than to know Jesus and make him known. But as we fight our own sin every day, we have an enemy who is doing everything he can to feed us lies so that we will question who we truly are to God. "Did God really say . . ." is the most misleading question in history.[13]

So I want you to stop right now and ask God with an honest heart, *Why would you want me?* Ask the Lord to show you anything that may be keeping you from true intimacy with him or any limiting beliefs you have about yourself that you feel disqualify you from working in partnership with him for the Kingdom. Then remember Tim Keller's gospel definition: "We are more loved and accepted in Jesus Christ than we ever dared hope."[14] Live from that truth today.

When Lucas pulled me aside on that dirt road and asked, "Why did you choose me?" I told him the truth—I'd chosen him because I'd been chosen too. I'd been pursued by radical, unearned love, because Jesus chooses the wildest mustangs. How could I do any less?

The next day, after the four rehabilitation participants had picked out and named their horses, the rest of the herd had to be shipped away. We sat on the top rail of the fence and watched the trailer full of unchosen mustangs drive away from the ranch to go back to the holding facilities, where the horses would likely spend the rest of their lives.

"Pfft, prison," Lucas said, shaking his head. "I don't understand why people would choose a regular horse over a wild one."

Landon responded, "Cause they're so much trouble to tame."

Landon and Lucas summed up the struggle of taming mustangs. And they knew from personal experience why the wild ones so often get passed over. That's why it's so meaningful that Jesus chooses the untamed and the bold.

Jesus could have assembled a dream team. If he wanted, he could have found the bravest, most capable, intellectual, and godly men. Instead, he stopped by the booth of a tax collector—a profession despised by everyone—and called Matthew to follow him. Then he approached a group of low-life fishermen and told them to drop their nets. He called Simon, a member of a revolutionary group, and asked him to join a movement far more radical than the one he was currently affiliated with. And this ragtag group was chosen to be the messengers who would go into the world and tell others about a Messiah who would save them from their sins. Why?

And it isn't just the choosing of the disciples that could make us scratch our heads in wonder.

Why Moses? He couldn't speak well, clearly had a temper, killed a guy and fled from Egypt, and didn't even want to go rescue his fellow Israelites from slavery, having all sorts of excuses when God said to go.[15] This is the same man who eventually led a million captives into freedom across a parted sea.[16]

Why Rahab? A known prostitute and the citizen of a city that God would soon destroy for its disobedience and irreverence, she had just enough faith to safely hide the Israelite spies. She had heard what their God had done, and she knew a God like that was the only God worth following.[17]

Why David? A young boy tending sheep in the fields, occasionally taking down a bear or a lion, he was anointed to become the king of Israel. This seemingly unqualified king was also an adulterous murderer, but in his repentance and worship, he was still called a man after God's own heart.[18]

Why Paul? A fierce opponent of the message of Christianity and ruthless persecutor of those following it, he was chosen by God to become one of the most prominent Christian missionaries and evangelists to walk the planet.[19]

Why did God choose these mustangs?

The answer is in the heart of Christ: meekness.

God is looking for warhorses he can lead into battle. And there are three qualities of meekness that are shared by all warhorses used by God.

1. **Warhorses are wild enough to answer the call of discipleship.** Risk-taking, bold, influential, all in—there is nothing lukewarm about mustangs. They are unfazed by the cacophony of war and are able to run straight into the heat of battle at their master's lead.
2. **Warhorses give full submission to their master.** Once they trust their leader's heart, mustangs are perfectly in tune with even the slightest nudge of the reigns or the smallest change in emotions. In an instant, warhorses will respond accordingly.

3. **Warhorses show us redemption.** God, from the beginning, creates ex nihilo, making something out of nothing. He raises dry bones to a standing army. He tames the wild, throwaway mustang into a warhorse and molds the seemingly irredeemable into someone purposeful for his Kingdom, something he alone could get the glory for.

Like the thousands of wild mustangs kept behind bars in holding facilities, the wild men and women of God are also behind bars. Bars of sin, shame, pride, misguided purpose, and misplaced identity. It's impossible to see a generation turn back to the Lord and learn the true strength of meekness if the wild ones don't understand their God-designed value. This was my story, in my misunderstanding of how God could use someone who didn't always fit the mold.

But I believe it is the prisoner who best understands the gift of freedom; it is the orphan who best understands family; it is the broken who best understands becoming whole. And I believe it is the mustang who best understands what it is to be meek, to have the radically countercultural strength to live with their eyes fixed on Jesus.

Mustangs are designed to be gentled into warhorses for the Kingdom of God. They are wild enough to answer the call and humble enough to submit to their master. And in their taming, God alone is glorified by showing his *prosdechomai* love and redemption for the most unlikely leaders. And that is exactly why God wants mustangs.

CHAPTER 3

THE BIT IN THE MOUTH

All this assembly may know that the LORD saves not with sword and spear. For the battle is the LORD's.

1 SAMUEL 17:47, ESV

Wild mustangs refuse to fit into any neat category we might like to put them in. They weigh up to one thousand pounds of pure muscle, with hooves made of keratin and bone and reflexes that could kick you in the face faster than you could think to move out of the way. It makes sense why a lot of people are afraid of them. Their entire posture and presence is unpredictable. When Lucas first met his mustang on the ranch, he commented, "I don't like these animals. My grandpa got his finger bit straight off by a horse." He looked fearfully down at his fingers, then back up at his horse. We all burst out laughing, but Lucas stayed a bit frozen at the thought of not having all ten of his fingers intact.

While they are animals that we should rightfully respect, mustangs are actually prey animals. They are the hunted far more than the hunter. They've got eyes on the sides of their heads to scan for predators like us, who have eyes in the front of our heads to look for prey to kill. For a wild, often vulnerable horse to submit and trust someone who could be a threat to them, like a human, is amazing when you think about it—and makes these giants seem a little gentler.

Mustangs are, by their nature, a paradox. Wild, reactive, capable of destruction and even death. Yet when gentled, they are humble, submissive, willing to run the rest of their lives for the one who trained them to trust.

As I learned more about mustangs and spent time with them on the ranch, I started to learn so much more about how God sees me. Grant, the trainer, said that mustangs were how he found God in the first place, and I can see why. There is so much beauty and mystery and honor found in the juxtaposition of their meek and wild natures. These animals taught me not only about God but about what it means to be a godly man, and at a pretty crucial time in my life to learn it.

I didn't hit puberty until it seemed like the rest of my friends had beards and girlfriends. In high school I was about 5'2" and weighed 120 pounds, but with no muscle in sight. I don't even know how that math works out, but I've got pictures to prove it. I also had a wild head of hair, and not in a good way. I've got the pictures to prove that too.

Because of those characteristics, I was an insecure teenager. There was a relentless barrage of derogatory words hurled my way. The combination of many of the cultural expectations around me, and my own experience of being made fun of, gave me an internal read on what it meant to be a man. But it wasn't a healthy perspective. Or a biblical one. I was off on the wrong trajectory of proving my worth before I even left home for college.

MISGUIDED PURSUIT

This desire to prove myself hit a breaking point in my junior year of college. My girlfriend of two years cheated on me with one of my best friends, causing me to go into the darkest place I had ever been. I felt duped, like someone had just taken all my confidence, ripped it to shreds, and left it in a pile on the ground. But because I had to keep my posture of toughness, I couldn't show the pain I was in. I had to act like the betrayal hadn't hurt me. My subconscious way of coping with it was to dive even deeper into proving myself to be what I thought was a real man. I was desperate to pick the pieces of my confidence off the ground and put it back together, so I went to the next level to show that nobody could ever take advantage of me like that again.

To start, because I felt stupid, I wanted to prove how smart I was. I walked into the registrar's office at my college and changed my double major in communications and Christian education to philosophy, the undisputed hardest major at the school. Since it was my junior year, I would need to take the maximum amount of credits in advanced classes every semester in order to graduate, but I didn't care. I did it anyway, because I was out to prove a point.

I felt vulnerable, so I started leading girls on, toying with their emotions, misleading their hearts and minds while knowing exactly what I was doing the whole time. I was trying to show that I could have the upper hand in a relationship. I didn't want to ever feel like I was powerless over what happened to me when I cared for someone again.

And because I felt weak, I started doing the most intense, unhealthy workouts in order to demonstrate my physical and mental toughness. I showed up and ran the Chicago Marathon without doing any training, having never run more than a few miles in my life. I finished, but not without my body taking a pretty heavy and painful hit, a foreshadowing of what the lifestyle I was living would continue to do. As a whole, I had made it my mission to become someone who nobody could take advantage of anymore by being smarter, savvier, and stronger. In my mind, those things were the key to respect.

After college, I started training to become a Navy SEAL, when I wasn't training for the minor league baseball season. I met a man named Riley (the same Riley who stood up for Lucas in the courtroom to get him to the ranch) who would take me to the beach and have me do ridiculous workouts that no one should ever do. Riley was not only a 6'5", 240-pound former Navy SEAL, but he was also a former drug dealer from the Bronx whose life was radically transformed by Jesus while he was in the military. He was one bad dude and the epitome of everything I wanted to be.

THE FIGHT THAT TURNED ME AROUND

One night, my friends and I went on a triple date to a major league baseball game. It was me; my best friend Nathan, who was a former heavyweight wrestler in college; and my friend Ben, a hipster writer from LA who had come to visit. As the night was winding down, we decided to go to a fast-food drive-through to get something to eat on our way home. It was a weekend, and most people downtown had been partying hard. Our car windows were down so we could enjoy the cool summer night. All seemed well until out of nowhere, a random guy approached the car and started throwing punches at my friend Ben through the rolled-down passenger-side window of the back seat. My body jolted in shock, quickly trying to understand what was going on.

The girls with us screamed as Ben took a beating. I jumped out of the car to help my friend, and the guy turned his attention to me, throwing a haymaker that I ducked before clocking him and sending him falling to the ground. As he got up, my friend Nathan, the heavyweight wrestler, threw me out of the way, squared up to the guy, and, full of adrenaline and anger, started yelling and taunting, "Hit me!"

The guy threw a punch at Nathan's face, but my friend was completely unphased. Then Nathan gave him a right hook that sent the guy flying again. No exaggeration, I watched this guy's teeth shoot out of his mouth and hit the pavement. It was bad. Soon, some of his friends ran to the scene, apologizing for their drunk friend, who had mistaken

Ben for someone else, and the brief fight was over almost as quickly as it had started. But as we got back in the car, I noticed Nathan clutching his hand. When he let us take a look, we saw that he had sliced his hand down to the bone on the teeth of the guy he had punched. I don't even know who I would say won the fight: the hand or the teeth. They were both in rough shape.

We dropped our shell-shocked dates at their homes, then rushed Nathan to the hospital, talking the whole way about how crazy the situation was. When we finally arrived at the emergency room, Nathan was rushed into surgery because apparently the mouth is the most germ-ridden place on the human body and, with the time that had passed, bacteria could have made it into his bloodstream. Luckily this wasn't the case, but it definitely freaked us out and added to the drama of the night.

In the aftermath of that night, I have to say that I was pretty proud of how we had defended our friend from an unjust attack. I couldn't wait to share with Riley how I had stood up for my buddy and for what was right. No one should get sucker punched at a drive-through, and we were not going to let it happen on our watch.

The next day, I met with Riley at his house and recounted the whole story. The blindside punch through the open back window. How quickly I got out of the car. The teeth on the ground. The stitches in Nathan's hand. It all felt so epic. And I knew that as a former SEAL who understands what brotherhood really means, Riley would be proud of me for defending Ben. I started telling him about the situation, sparing no detail and probably playing up how heroic I felt to get the guy off of my friend. But Riley just stared blankly at me.

Confused, and not liking the awkward silence that followed my story, I rambled off some disclaimers about how it was self-defense and we didn't have a choice, but Riley put his hand in the air and cut me off.

"Could you have de-escalated that situation?"

"Uhh, what do you mean?" I responded in confusion.

"Was there a way you could have de-escalated that situation without continuing to get violent?"

Now keep in mind, Riley had just left the SEAL team where he had been deployed overseas several times. He had seen and done some risky stuff in his day, stuff that he rarely mentioned and certainly never bragged about—real stories of tense and dangerous situations where life and death were at stake. Riley knew what it meant to fight for something. And when to fight.

Still confused by Riley's response of correction that I hadn't been anticipating, I remained silent. Riley could tell that I was not getting his point, so he let out a frustrated exhale and began to explain.

"Here's what I mean, man: The other day I was at the veterans hospital visiting a buddy of mine. As I was leaving, I pulled out of my parking space and almost got T-boned by a lowrider car with spinning rims that was recklessly speeding through the parking lot. He swerved out of the way, and I hit the brakes, as we narrowly missed each other. It was clearly his fault. I watched in my side mirror as this little wannabe thug with baggy pants and tattoos covering his whole body started cussing at me from his car. The dude kept freaking out and even got out of his car, stomping his way over to mine. *Here we go*, I thought. He pounded his fists on my window, signaling for me to get out of the car."

This was the part of the story where I got excited. Riley could take on anyone, and my hunch was that he could snap this little jerk with his pinkie. "What did you do to him?" I interrupted.

"I rolled down my window and apologized, 'Hey, so sorry, man, I didn't see you there. Please forgive me.'"

"You did what?" I shouted at the injustice.

"Yeah, man. I asked him to forgive me."

"And?"

"And he got the funniest look on his face, scratched his head, then shook my hand, saying, 'Yeah, man, all good.' Then he walked back to his car. That's what I mean by de-escalating a situation. Could a different reaction last night have meant that no one lost his teeth and no one needed surgery?"

I left my time with Riley the slightest bit disoriented but refreshed at the same time. I certainly didn't feel proud of my fight anymore. This man who I deeply respected, the one I wanted to be like in so many ways, had just caused a paradigm shift in how I viewed strength, justice, self-defense, loyalty, and toughness. I thought the person who proves their worth is the one who wins the fight. Turns out the one worth anything is the guy who stops the fight before it starts.

There was something so radical and refreshing about Riley's perspective that it convicted me to the core. It was a new category for me and certainly wasn't a posture I had been seeking. I wanted to prove how much smarter and stronger I could be than everyone else. If you're trying to be the best, brightest, and baddest, why would you look to be the gentlest? The two dispositions didn't seem to fit together.

When taming a wild mustang, one of the first steps after the horse lets you come near him is to get the horse to open his mouth, because you have to put a bit—the small piece of equipment that guides the horse—inside. You can't ride, further train, or put the horse to much constructive use without having a bit in his mouth. But a wild mustang isn't going to just let this happen. He might let you come near him after painstakingly working with eye contact and earning his trust, but before he is going to willingly open his mouth, the horse has to learn to slow down, control his default reaction to run, and be still enough for this vital step.

Riley was teaching me, in real time, the same lesson.

Where I had merely reacted to my situation, Riley had thoughtfully responded to his. And my enthusiasm in bragging about my toughness was lost on a true man of war, who had all the capacity to unleash his power yet held it back. It wasn't that he wasn't capable. Far from it. Riley had grown up as a wild mustang, finding trouble at every corner, using whatever means necessary to ensure no one else got the best of him. But through years of humbling in the military, and years of submitting to his Lord, Riley had become gentled, and a greater warrior than before. Because he had let the Lord guide him, Riley was ready to be led not by his emotions and desires but by a gentle and lowly King.

MEEK MOMENT

Have you ever rehearsed a fake argument in the shower or in the car—drumming up a tense scenario that never existed and then firing a zinger toward your imaginary adversary that really puts them in their place? Maybe you, like me, have given yourself an excuse for knocking someone's teeth out: a boss, a family member, a stranger on the internet. No matter the shape your frustration has taken, in some form, maybe you've wanted to take revenge into your own hands. What would it look like to invite Jesus into the situation instead of reacting in anger?

THE WAY OF SURRENDER

The more I study the men Jesus chose to be his closest followers, the more I am convinced that Jesus was looking for wild mustangs who could be tamed into warhorses. He wasn't looking for the smartest or the most spiritual. He wasn't looking for the guys with the greatest following, and he certainly didn't care about social influence. There were few people less popular in first-century Jewish culture than tax collectors like Matthew. Jesus was looking for mustangs who would be wild enough to run into battle yet gentle and attentive enough that they could learn to stop, be still, and allow Jesus to use their lives for whatever Kingdom-minded mission was next. He was looking for men that most would cast off to the side but whose outcast natures gave them the humility to sacrifice their rights and desires in favor of his.

No one is too wild to follow the Lord. David killed so many men and had so much blood on his hands that God wouldn't allow him to build the Temple.[1] Men like James and John wanted to command fire to rain down from heaven to kill the Samaritans who had rejected Jesus.[2] And men like Paul and Simon the Zealot were terrorists, but when their radical and wild natures were redirected, they answered the call of discipleship with their full selves and full lives.

It is impossible to find a lukewarm follower of Jesus. Jesus came for the mustangs who often recklessly kicked and bucked but who also had the most tender heart for him. King David was ridiculed for singing and dancing to God, only to respond by saying, "I will become even more undignified than this."[3] The apostle John had the gentleness to lay his head on Jesus' chest.[4] And, of course, Paul vulnerably and openly debated whether it was better to be in heaven with Jesus or to continue suffering on earth for his sake so that others could know him.[5] All of these men were the picture of a paradox. But maybe none of them were more paradoxical than Peter.

Throughout the Gospels, it seems like nobody was more in love with Jesus than Peter. He was one of the disciples who was closest to Jesus, yet he often got himself into trouble with his brashness and tendency to speak before thinking. I'm convinced, however, that this is why Jesus loved him so much. Peter was a mustang through and through, and he just needed to let Jesus tame his wild heart. No doubt, Jesus had to turn up the heat on him, even famously telling him, "Get behind me, Satan!"[6] Strong words for someone you love dearly.

Jesus was always trying to teach Peter meekness, while Peter kicked and bucked him each step of the way. To see the clearest depiction of meekness versus recklessness, look no farther than the garden of Gethsemane, where Judas betrayed Jesus, delivering him over to the chief priests, soldiers, and Pharisees to be arrested. The account in John 18 shows us the scene:

> When he had finished praying, Jesus left with his disciples and crossed the Kidron Valley. On the other side there was a garden, and he and his disciples went into it.
>
> Now Judas, who betrayed him, knew the place, because Jesus had often met there with his disciples. So Judas came to the garden, guiding a detachment of soldiers and some officials from the chief priests and the Pharisees. They were carrying torches, lanterns and weapons.
>
> Jesus, knowing all that was going to happen to him, went out and asked them, "Who is it you want?"

> "Jesus of Nazareth," they replied.
>
> "I am he," Jesus said. (And Judas the traitor was standing there with them.)
>
> When Jesus said, "I am he," they drew back and fell to the ground.
>
> Again he asked them, "Who is it you want?"
>
> "Jesus of Nazareth," they said.
>
> Jesus answered, "I told you that I am he. If you are looking for me, then let these men go." This happened so that the words he had spoken would be fulfilled: "I have not lost one of those you gave me."
>
> Then Simon Peter, who had a sword, drew it and struck the high priest's servant, cutting off his right ear. (The servant's name was Malchus.)
>
> Jesus commanded Peter, "Put your sword away! Shall I not drink the cup the Father has given me?"[7]

Meekness is living with a bit in your mouth, keeping the sword in the sheath, knowing whose battle it truly is. Peter drew a sword, but Jesus knocked it to the ground with a single sentence.

No matter how erratic and imperfect Peter could be, he was in love with his Lord. Jesus used his disposition to help bring the gospel to the ends of the earth. Peter learned to come close to his teacher, to trust that what Jesus would do next was always going to be right. I'm sure that everything in Peter was screaming, "No! There is a better, smarter, stronger way to bring your Kingdom to earth, Jesus! We don't have to be this gentle!" I think Peter, too, might have been the first one out of the car to defend his friend from getting hit in the back seat.

Yet Jesus, out of the meekness in his heart, his Father's strength under control, simply says to Peter, "No, Peter, there's no need to fight. *My surrender is the way.* No one needs to lose an ear tonight, because I'm going to lose my life for many."

Surrendering to Jesus is a discipline every one of us needs to practice. Can you take a minute and pray for discernment before commenting on that social media post that bothered you, asking the Lord if that is really your battle to fight, if you really have something important to prove? Can you slow down your response when you think your spouse has wronged you before coming up with all sorts of skewed evidence that he or she is not really on your side? Can you remember your own imperfections and growth, and all the moments you've needed correction, before letting all your anger out on your teenager for making a poor decision? Our words and actions can be a weapon for the right fight, but weapons also hurt people. Meek men and women understand that choosing surrender demonstrates the character of someone who realizes their own need for forgiveness, someone who has relinquished the right to take vengeance and left that to God. And yet that choice to surrender is the surest sign of strength.

MEEK MOMENT

Close your eyes and hold out your hands like you're holding a bowl. Imagine all the weight of the offenses you've felt toward you—every harsh word, every manipulation, every way you've felt taken advantage of. Hold that weight in front of you and look to Jesus.

Now say this prayer, filling in the blanks:

Jesus, I relinquish my right to take revenge against ____________ (their name) for ____________ (how I feel wronged). I bless them in the name of Jesus with peace, wisdom, and clarity.

Breathe deeply. Trust that justice belongs to the Lord and that he will deal with the offenses. They are not your responsibility, so let the weight fall off your shoulders. And remember Jesus' encouragement that the peacemakers are blessed, for they will be called children of God.[8]

REAL WORTH

For much of my life, I had been asking myself, "What is a godly man?" and "Am I that?" I was in a game of ping-pong, bouncing back and forth between the tough, domineering type of strength I had seen in popular culture and the kind of gentleness I sensed in the heroes of the Bible. At the time, I wanted to be the type of guy who could walk into a room and have people go, "Whoa, don't mess with him." Even if you don't relate to the desire to be seen as tough, maybe you've wanted to be considered intellectual, popular, or attractive. I think many of us spend so much of our lives trying to figure out what it means to be the most admired version of ourselves. It's part of our default mode to care too much about what people think of us.

For me, when I followed the world's ideas about strength, trying to impress others, the God-given fire inside me started to burn people. Soon, teachers couldn't stand me, coaches couldn't control me, and my parents didn't know what to do with me. Every time I screwed up, the authority figure in that situation would do their best to convince me that my behavior was not okay and then punish me for acting out. This is completely reasonable. Caring authorities do correct mistakes.

But so often, I felt like people were not merely trying to discipline me—they were trying to change me. They didn't see the wild in me as something that could be used for good but as a character trait that needed to be crushed.

When Riley modeled for me not just strength and power but humility and restraint, it hit me in a deep part of my soul that longed for an example like his, one that I knew in my gut was the truest form of manhood. It wasn't the tough-guy version of punching someone out in a parking lot. And it wasn't someone refusing to take any action at all. It was pure meekness. Eyes off yourself and on others. Strength under control.

Many of us think of a man after God's own heart as someone who writes his own worship songs and keeps eloquent journal entries.[9] And that very well could be true. There is not one formula for what it looks like to be a follower of Christ in the world. After all, David played the harp, worshiped God with abandon, *and* killed bears, lions, and giants. I had to learn over the years, in my conversations with some of the meekest people on earth, that boldness has many dispositions. I believe the God-given fire inside of us is what drives believers to be radically on mission to spread the gospel wherever we are. To harness our first reactions, come close to Jesus, and let him put the bit in our mouths so he can guide us to what is next.

Once we can learn to do that, to be still before the Lord, we can listen to the whispers of the Holy Spirit, the ones that are so easily drowned out by the noise in the world and the many things vying for our attention. If meekness is our goal, our spiritual hearing must be clear. God-given wildness doesn't naturally respond to nudges, but a tamed mustang does.

CHAPTER 4

THE NUDGE OF THE REINS

My sheep listen to my voice; I know them, and they follow me.

JOHN 10:27

There's something sacred about the first moments of taming a wild mustang. You don't start with touch; you start with presence. You stand still long enough for him to see you, to know you're not a threat. Then comes the look—eye to eye. Two creatures, both unsure, both waiting.

He flinches. You stay. He tests your silence. You don't move. And then, for the first time, he doesn't turn away. In that brief meeting of eyes, something shifts. The fight softens, not all at once, but enough to make room for trust. Only then do you take a step, not to conquer but to come closer. The air feels fragile, like one wrong move could shatter it. You breathe slower than you ever have. He watches. You wait. Trust, it turns out, isn't built by force—it's born in patience.

Days later, each inch of trust has been earned by the consistency of your presence. He lets you place the halter on, then the bit. The sound of the leather settling against his skin is almost holy. The wild that once refused the reins now listens to them. They call this "breaking" the horse. But he's not broken; he's become willing. The power is still there, but it's a peaceful power now. A yielded strength that is ready to hear what his master has for him.

It takes time and consistency and love to show a horse how to follow orders with only a gentle nudge of the reins, but the miracle is that he does. He learns to respond to every single pull and hint of pressure. The horse that was once terrified, dangerous, and out of control can become a loyal, fearless, submissive warrior once he learns what it means to listen.

AGAPE

During my time with Landon, Caleb, Dawson, and Lucas at the ranch, each of them had the chance to pick one mustang that they wanted to work with for the next few months. None of them knew anything about horses, much less about how to train a wild one. They were raised in urban neighborhoods with few resources. They grew up being told stories about how to survive on the streets, not about the Wild West—so they were all choosing based on first impressions and intuition.

Caleb was a tough-on-the-outside, gentle-on-the-inside young man from California. He was someone I believed in with everything I had—and that's still true today. When it was time to choose a mustang, Caleb stood outside the round pens and watched the horses patiently, not certain of how to pick. But one horse kept coming back to mind for him: the wildest, scariest, most intimidating horse we had.

In the mornings, when we would visit the round pens, we would often see this specific horse's pen in disarray, the aluminum poles of the corral dented and bent, like someone had been trying to run them over from the inside. That someone was a horse who'd spent hours and hours angrily trying to break free with his head and hind legs.

"That's the one I want," Caleb told us, pointing to the furious animal.

"You sure, bro?" I asked him, knowing that taming *any* mustang would be a tall order but taming *this one* could be a recipe for failure. And I did not want any of these young men to fail.

"I'm sure," Caleb insisted. "That one."

The horse Caleb wanted terrified all of us. He was a large, dark brown mustang, with wild, angry eyes popping out of his skull, as if he lived in a constant state of fear and restlessness. He wanted out, back to the wild, away from anyone who came near him. He breathed heavily, constantly snorting in frustration and giving absolutely no indication he was going to glance in anyone's direction, much less trust them.

The program participants all had the chance to name their horses. Caleb, who is Salvadorian, chose *Toro*, which means "bull" in Spanish.

"Toro," I said back to him and chuckled. "That seems fitting, honestly. This guy looks like he might be more bull than horse anyway."

But as Caleb nodded along to my banter, something in his body shifted. He kept his eyes on Toro, but I could see he was thinking deeply about the name he'd picked. Then he finally spoke up. "You know," Caleb said, "I don't think I want to name this horse based on who he is right now but based on who he's going to be." This was a powerful decision coming from a young man who had already been labeled by the world for who he was in his worst moments.

"Everyone says I should pick a different horse, but I'm not going to," Caleb told me. This was true, because I was one of the people openly second-guessing his choice. "I'm going to work with this one. And his name is Agape."

Agapē is the Greek word for unconditional love.[1] And not just that, but *agapē* is also used to describe God's love for humanity: selfless, sacrificial, not motivated by feelings but simply by, well, love. There are other words for love in the Greek language: *philia*,[2] which refers to the love between friends; *eros*,[3] meaning romantic love; and *storgē*,[4] which is the love among family members. But *agapē* is different, bigger—a perfect and unwavering love. A love for the wild, the untamed, the forgotten. For the mustangs.

After choosing Agape, Caleb was out there in the round pen for hours and hours, sometimes questioning his choice and feeling like his efforts to connect with this horse were futile.

But over time, Agape started to change. His posture relaxed a little, and then a lot. The poles holding his round pen together weren't dented anymore. His breathing slowed. And the thing everyone noticed about Agape, from the ranch hands to the other participants, was that his eyes changed completely. When Caleb first chose Agape, the mustang's eyes were protruding and large. Over time, they seemed to get smaller, fully at ease. Agape wasn't scared anymore, wasn't dangerously trying to run away. He simply wasn't the same horse, and we all saw it in his eyes.

This horse was not made to be autonomous, using his God-given strength only to run wild and try to stay alive. Instead, he was created for a purpose, and his purpose was found in having a master he trusted. When Caleb was able to get his heart, Agape could finally settle into the role he was made for. Agape could finally rest.

So many of us chase freedom from submission because we think that is where happiness and contentment will be found, but the opposite is true. Submission and surrender to the one who made us, who has already written the perfect plan for our lives, is the key to meekness, which is what will bring us true rest. As Saint Augustine famously said, "You have made us for yourself, [Lord,] and our hearts are restless until they rest in You."[5]

Letting go of control over your life—or I should say, the little you actually can control—feels scary, until you realize that the one who has control is perfect. And he always has been. His love is the foundation of everything we are and everything we can be. Like Agape, when we stop running, we find the rest we've been looking for all along.

ASKING PERMISSION

There are few people in Scripture who displayed obedient submission as much as King David. David often explicitly asked the Lord for guidance in specific ways. Even before he took Saul's place as the leader of Israel, David had made it a consistent habit of his prayer life to inquire of the Lord.[6]

In 1 Samuel 30, David returned home from fighting under the command of Achish against the Philistines to the city of Ziklag to find that his city had been attacked, pillaged, and burned. His entire family, as well as the families of other men, had been taken captive by the Amalekites. Scripture tells us that "David and his men wept aloud until they had no strength left to weep."[7]

The situation was dire. Not only were David's men weak with grief over the loss of their families, but they needed to do something with their pain. As many of us tend to do, David's men wanted to blame someone, and they directed their anger at David. They began to talk of stoning him to death, as if it would relieve the impossible angst of their own hurt to hurt someone else.

But David, as he had learned to do long before this moment, turned to God. He prayed to the Lord and begged for guidance on his next steps. It wasn't simply a "help me to do your will, God" kind of prayer. There was no ambiguity in David's petitions before the Lord. With the boldness that can only come from intimacy with the one you are asking permission from, David said, "Shall I pursue this raiding party?" Then he followed that question with another clear one: "Will I overtake them?"[8] *Do you want me to go after these offenders, God? Is my next step an act of bold pursuit? If I do go, will it work?*

And the Lord told him, "Pursue them. You will certainly overtake them and succeed in the rescue."[9]

Scripture does not tell us how David went back to the men who wanted to kill him or how he was able to convince them to follow him into another battle. They were weary and exhausted. They'd been moving from one battle to the next for months. Here, they were also leveled with grief over their plundered city and lost families, while being expected to trust that the Lord had spoken to their leader, who told them to get on their feet and fight again.

Not all of them had the strength to do so. But four hundred men, led by David, found the Amalekites in the countryside—basically having a big party to celebrate what they had just done to their enemy's homes. David and his men not only overtook them but recovered everything the Amalekites had taken, including their families.[10]

David had prayed to the Lord for guidance, but he was not seeking self-protection or self-promotion. He simply trusted that the Lord would tell him exactly what he should do. In David's inquiries of the Lord, he was really asking three kinds of questions:

1. *Should I go?* Is this the right path?
2. *Will it work?* Will I be successful?
3. *How should I do it?* What is the method you want me to use?

David's willingness to ask these questions and let the Lord guide his specific steps exemplifies a heart fully surrendered to God.

MEEK MOMENT

God is always speaking—always whispering, always nudging the reins. Our inability to hear him at times has nothing to do with his presence. Even in the noise of our world, he still speaks, and we can hear him when we listen with intention. In Isaiah 30:21, he promises us, "Your ears will hear a voice behind you, saying, 'This is the way, walk in it.'" Take a silent moment sometime today to listen for God's voice.

NOT JUST FOR KINGS

Honest, vulnerable prayers to God are not just a thing of the Old Testament—nor are answers, guidance, and promptings reserved for a select group of holy people. If we look to the Gospels, we can see that the biggest requirement for Jesus to move in someone's life is trust in him. The wedding that ran out of wine? Jesus' mother knew the hosts' reputations were at stake, and she asked Jesus to change the trajectory of the whole event.[11] The woman with the issue of blood? She had exhausted every other option for healing, so she went all in on a man she had only heard of when she reached for the hem of his garment. She had nothing but the belief that he *could* heal her.[12] The men who wanted their paralyzed friend healed? To get close to Jesus, they cut a hole in the roof.[13] All of them were bold enough to approach Jesus and meek enough to acknowledge their need for him and trust his will.

Jamie Winship, a former police officer and Christian evangelist and author, was once in a unit tasked with searching for missing children. In this role, Jamie not only had to beg for God's hand of justice, but he had to learn to lean heavily on the nudges of the Holy Spirit. When he was involved in these tense and scary situations, he would ask the Holy Spirit to help him see something no human eye could see. On one search, the Lord nudged Jamie toward a specific car. Though on any other day nothing would have caused a police officer to stop the vehicle, Jamie felt undeniably prompted to pull the car over. The child he was looking for was in that very car.[14]

Two women I consider heroes of the faith, my friends Marziyeh and Maryam, were both held in Iran's Evin Prison—infamously nicknamed the "Torture Factory"—for secretly passing out Bibles all over the city of Tehran. These two women had a long history of trusting the Lord for otherworldly courage, and in prison, this pattern of trusting the whispers of the Holy Spirit saved their lives.

The Iranian regime threatened to have them executed, but more than once the women heard clear directives from the Lord and heeded them. The Holy Spirit would tell them to pray for a specific guard, and that evening the guard would have a dream in which God told him not to touch the two women. God's miraculous provision followed the surrendered prayers of these heroes, and their lives were ultimately spared.[15]

One of the most inspiring stories I've heard, at least when it comes to asking the Lord for guidance and listening to his voice, is from another woman, Aja Brown. Aja is a mentor, friend, prayer warrior, and sister in Christ who was told by the Holy Spirit in her prayer time that she was going to be the mayor of Compton, California, when she was only thirty years old. Government leadership is not easy on any level or in any location, but Compton is a uniquely complicated city. Crime, gang activity, and heavy racial division are deeply embedded in the city's history. Aja, who had moved to Compton to take on a role as a project manager for the city, would often drive through town praying for the flourishing of places many folks avoided. One day during her prayer time, after witnessing corruption in leadership, she asked God who might be the best person to lead the city next. She wanted to get that answer from God and throw her full support behind whoever he revealed to her.

But God must have shaken his head at Aja with a chuckle, thinking, *Just wait*. Because Aja clearly heard the Lord say, "I brought *you* here to be the next mayor of Compton," and then he gave her a blueprint for how to run her campaign and a slogan to go with it: "New Vision for Compton." That's it. That's the phrase the Lord gave her to sum up her entire campaign. Not "Aja Brown for Mayor" or anything with her name on it. Every marketing professional and political campaigner would have told her, "You can't run for mayor without putting your name out there." But Aja did not budge. "The Lord told me it's going to be 'New Vision for Compton,' and people will know," she said.[16]

After getting out on the streets and visiting citizens, asking real community members about their pain points and desires for their city, Aja ultimately won the mayoral race in a landslide. During her tenure, with the vision she developed by listening to the people and communing with God about how to tackle the problems in front of her, Aja saw unemployment drop from 21 percent to 4 percent.[17] A handful of new grocery stores opened, and the area was no longer considered a food desert.* Members from two prominent and violent gangs, the Bloods and Crips, gathered together regularly with Aja to talk about what kind of a city they wanted to leave for their kids.[18] Seemingly impossible bonds of peace were forged through those tearful, honest meetings between men who sometimes grew up on the same street but had become sworn enemies. Aja's eight years as the mayor of Compton were nothing short of miraculous. All because she listened to the nudges.

---

* A "food desert" is an area in which it is difficult to buy affordable or good-quality fresh food.

Finding a missing child in a random vehicle; seeing prison guards walk away from unarmed, imprisoned women; being elected to cast a new vision for a hurting city without putting your name on any campaign signs—none of this makes logical sense: It doesn't fit into our strategies for success. But the things we think we can achieve in our strength are actually the very things that blind us to what God can really do. When we reach the limit of our own abilities, God makes miracles happen.

Learning to ask God for guidance and being able to follow the nudge of his reins leads to the kind of adventure we couldn't have imagined if we had continued relying on our own wisdom and strength. God desires to speak to us, to give us clarity for the next steps in our lives, to use us in every situation he has prepared for us. He is a God of intention, moving us here and there in a manner that we will never fully understand this side of eternity, but if we quiet our hearts and ask him to guide us, he delights to do so.

So let's consider this question: When was the most recent time in your life that you heard from the Holy Spirit?

You've probably asked about big things—should I take this job, marry this person, move to that city?— but you don't have a divine Helper simply to make good decisions that only come along a few times in life. You have a Helper for *today*. For right now. For this moment. You have a Helper for later this morning, when you pick up your coffee at Starbucks and wonder if you should ask the barista how she's doing. For this afternoon, when your house is in total chaos and you want to yell but instead ask the Lord for the ability to see your kids with his patience. For tonight, when you might be tempted to watch something you shouldn't and ask for a conviction that won't even let you pick up your phone. Inviting the Holy Spirit into the mundane and everyday moments of life only makes him clearer in the big ones. But really, when you think about it, isn't every day of your life a big day when God is using you for his Kingdom work?

We will never master the art of listening to the Holy Spirit, but we can drown out the noise around us and learn to hear him more often. It's not going to come naturally; it will be a challenge. But living in response to the prompting of the Lord is the only way to truly live in peace. Heeding the Spirit is a near constant reminder that we are not in control. To invite God into your thoughts at every opportunity is to trust that the one holding the reins will take you places only he can.

MEEK MOMENT

I'm sure there are specific decisions, questions, and next steps in your life that you're seeking clarity on. Take a minute now and get quiet. No phones, no notifications, no distractions between you and the one you need to hear from. Ask the Lord to speak into your circumstances with his still, small voice, nudging you in the direction you should go. Get specific and don't be afraid to ask with bold faith. If you need help getting started, pray this prayer:

Lord, help me to be still and wait for you: for your leading, for the subtle but undeniable nudge of your direction in my life. You are always doing a new thing, God, and I don't want to miss it because I wasn't listening. May your whispers rise above every sound in my life.

Amen.

FINISHING STRONG

King Asa, who was the great-great-grandson of King David, started his reign over Judah strong. He was the kind of king you'd want to root for—he tore down idols, rebuilt the Lord's altar, and led his people back to a covenant with God.[19] When a million-man Ethiopian army rose against him, Asa didn't flinch. He didn't scramble for alliances or draw up clever strategies. He cried out, "Lord, there is no one like you to help the powerless against the mighty. . . . We rely on you."[20] And God delivered him.

But somewhere along the way, Asa stopped seeking the Lord.

Years later, when faced with another threat—this time from Israel—he didn't pray. He didn't pause. He took matters into his own hands. He emptied the treasuries, bought an alliance with Syria, and called it wisdom. From the outside, his actions probably looked strategic. Responsible. But from God's perspective? It was rebellion. Not a loud, visible rebellion—but the quiet kind that creeps in when trust gives way to control.

So the Lord sent the prophet Hanani to confront him: "You relied on the king of Aram and not on the LORD your God."[21] Asa's response? He doesn't break. He doesn't repent. He gets offended and throws the prophet in prison.[22] The same king who once cried out in desperation shuts his ears to correction.

The verse that follows still haunts me: "Even in his illness he did not seek help from the LORD, but only from the physicians."[23] Asa's body was sick, but it was his spirit that had gone numb. His ears were no longer tuned to God's voice. He had once walked by faith—but somewhere along the way, he started walking by arrogance and self-reliance.

Compare that to what we know about King David. He was another flawed man, but he had a different posture. David never outgrew the need to ask for guidance. When the Philistines came, he inquired of the Lord. And when they came again—same enemy, same place—he asked a second time. God gave him a completely different strategy.[24] David could have assumed that because he had "been there, done that" in a similar circumstance, there was no need to pause and get quiet enough to hear the Lord. But he didn't. He inquired of the Lord again.

That's what meekness really is. Not passivity. Not fragility. But power that stays soft. Strength that submits. Vulnerability that stays surrendered. Hard-earned wisdom that seeks discernment. A wild mustang tamed by the nudge of the reins.

David didn't always get it right. But his reflex when he was spiritually healthy was always "Lord, what do you want?" That was his compass. Not momentum, experience, or public opinion. Just "What do you want, God?"

This is what most people miss. Starting strong is easy. Charisma can get you some measure of worldly success. Grit can get you résumé builders. A good launch season, a passionate moment of revival, an emotional altar call—they can all light the match. But finishing well? That's rare. Because finishing well requires the kind of long-term dependence that most people can't sustain. They trade it for self-reliance, for shortcut strategies, for doing what "makes sense." They simply stop asking for help.

But the ones who finish well never stop listening to the Lord. They never graduate from needing direction. They stay interruptible. They stay yielded. They stay meek.

Jesus said, "My sheep hear my voice, and I know them, and they follow me."[25] That's the whole deal right there. The mark of someone walking in step with the Spirit isn't their gifting—it's their ability to hear.

Psalm 32:8 says, "I will instruct you and teach you in the way you should go; I will counsel you with my loving eye on you." That's intimacy. That's not a drill sergeant barking commands. That's a Shepherd leading with presence. A Father guiding with a whisper.

And here's the promise: You will never go wrong asking God what he wants. Never. Even if you don't get an immediate answer. Even if it feels like silence. Even if you have to wait. If you make meekness your default setting—*What do you want from me, Lord?*—you will finish well. Because God finishes everything he authors, and he leads those who are willing to be led.

That's the kind of meekness I want. Not a life that looks powerful on paper—but a life that stays close enough to hear the whisper. A life where strength is real but yielded. A heart that never stops longing for the Holy Spirit to guide it.

That's how you finish well. That's the nudge of the reins.

CHAPTER 5

HIDDEN AND HOLY

All those who exalt themselves will be humbled, and those who humble themselves will be exalted.

LUKE 14:11

You know what's intimidating? Asking your boss for a promotion. Even if you've worked hard and clearly demonstrated your value to your organization. Even if you're well qualified. Even if you've put your time in, earned your bonuses, and garnered the respect of your colleagues. Even with everything in place, it takes a deep breath and some gusto to knock on your boss's door and ask, "Do you have a minute to chat?"

But at least you didn't send your mom to make the tough ask for you, right?

We can't say the same for two of the disciples we've come to know and love, the brothers James and John. Matthew 20:20-28 tells the story:

> The mother of the sons of Zebedee came up to him [Jesus] with her sons, and kneeling before him she asked him for something. And he said to her, "What do you want?"
>
> She said to him, "Say that these two sons of mine are to sit, one at your right hand and one at your left, in your kingdom."
>
> Jesus answered, "You do not know what you are asking. Are you able to drink the cup that I am to drink?"
>
> They said to him, "We are able."
>
> He said to them, "You will drink my cup, but to sit at my right hand and at my left is not mine to grant, but it is for those for whom it has been prepared by my Father."
>
> And when the ten heard it, they were indignant at the two brothers. But Jesus called them to him and said, "You know that the rulers of the Gentiles lord it over them, and their great ones exercise authority over them. It shall not be so among you. *But whoever would be great among you must be your servant, and whoever would be first among you must be your slave*, even as the Son of Man came not to be served but to serve, and to give his life as a ransom for many."[1]

I picture the scene and almost cringe a little, seeing grown-up James and John acting like two giddy boys hiding behind their mother's legs, fingers crossed, peeking around her to see Jesus' response.

These are the same young men who, sometime before this interaction, were walking with Jesus through Samaria, where "the people did not receive him, because his face was set toward Jerusalem."[2] The Samaritans, already unfriendly neighbors with the Jews, rejected Jesus. In James and John's indignation and thirst for retaliation, they asked Jesus, "Lord, do you want us to tell fire to come down from heaven and consume them?"[3]

It was a bit aggressive, even more impulsive, and pretty bold to ask the one who created fire whether he wanted them to use the power of his name, which he had bestowed on them, to take out an entire city. But these were the men Jesus had chosen to be his disciples, and I would argue that he chose them *for* their brash and wild impulsiveness, because he knew that spirit could be tamed into something meek and useful for Kingdom work.

Jesus turned to the brothers, gave them a quick rebuke—probably something like "You guys are wild. Calm down. There will be no fire today"—and then continued down the road with them.[4] I like to think of Jesus turning from James to John, shaking his head, and maybe chuckling to himself a bit, much like I do when my son does something completely ridiculous yet hilarious. Jesus gave these brothers what I think is the most awesome nickname in history, the "Sons of Thunder," a nod to not only their fiery plans but also their fiery personalities.[5]

But here they were, after they wanted to call down fire from heaven, and the Sons of Thunder were hiding behind their mom as she asked the question that truly had no place being asked at all: "Can my sons share the throne with you in heaven?"

Like Jesus often did, he responded with a question, directed not at their mother but at James and John and *their* desire for glory: "Are you able to suffer with me?" He was telling them, in other words, that in the Kingdom of God, glory doesn't come from your position on a stage but in proportion to the amount of suffering and lowliness you walk in.

On impulse, James and John both responded with an emphatic *yes*, but they still didn't get the point Jesus was trying to make. They couldn't have, because like the rest of the disciples, neither of them believed that Jesus would really die, much less die a gruesome criminal's death.

It's easy to *say* we are willing to give up anything to follow Jesus. But when push comes to shove, it's much harder to *live* that out. Jesus told the disciples that what really makes someone great is giving of themselves for the sake of others, not where they will sit in heaven. That won't matter much once we have a true taste of God's glory. Instead, we have to, like John the Baptist said, be willing to decrease so Jesus might increase.[6]

Years later, after witnessing the death and resurrection of Jesus, after being tamed and gentled through obedience, waiting, suffering, persecution, and perseverance, the two brothers would understand the meaning of meekness. James was faithful to the end and was the first disciple to be martyred.[7] John lived the longest of the original twelve disciples and penned some of the most beautiful words we have about selfless love. But first, these men had to be the mustangs who wanted Jesus to rain fire from heaven and who put their mother up to asking him for more glory. They, in their youth, thought that glory came from elevation. They quickly learned just how wrong they were. I can definitely relate.

MEEK MOMENT

Throughout my life, pastors, coaches, and teachers have seen my wildness, ambition, and desire for more and tried to squash it. I can understand why. But those of us who are mustangs bring a boldness that is vital to the church.

If you think that meekness means insignificance, let me tell you it doesn't. The wild ones can be truly tamed by God. Those with deep fire in their bones can become carriers of his flame. Only a Peter could stand at Pentecost. Only an Esther could stand before the king. Only a Moses could stand before Pharaoh. But it takes meekness to become truly great.

BRANDED

When I was a youth pastor in my mid-twenties, I longed to prove my worth to the "big boys" on the main stage. I knew

I could bring the house down with an epic, inspirational sermon that cut to the core of the congregation, leaving them longing for more of Jesus. I couldn't understand why the lead pastors kept bringing in guest speakers, who from my vantage point were boring people to tears, when I was readily available and willing to preach on a Sunday morning.

Occasionally, I was permitted to lead the offering or Communion during the Sunday service, and I would jump at the chance to get on stage. Over time, I began to turn those brief moments of asking the ushers to pass around the offering plate or explaining before Communion that "this is Christ's body, broken for you" into mini sermons. I would go on about the significance of tithing or the beauty of the symbol of Christ's sacrifice found in the grape juice and the bread. It was my time to shine, to elevate my status in the church, and I took every chance to show what I could do.

I began to study pastors of megachurches, watching how they paced the stage and structured their sermons. I even took note of how they dressed. I envied Christian celebrities, who seemed to have it all: a mission, respect, and fame. Then I noticed the wave of influencers with their massive audiences and followings, their capacity for marketing promotions, book deals, and speaking engagements. It was everything I envied.

When the idea for the rehabilitation program and the accompanying documentary started to grow, I can say with honesty that I did have at least some pure intentions. I did want to inspire people to see the heart of the mustang, and

I did want to share the gospel. But there is no doubt that I also wanted renown. I believed that if we did it right, the program's reach would be far greater than a five-minute mini sermon about tithing, delivered to a congregation of three hundred. I would be the wise mentor giving help and guidance to these boys on the ranch, all while sharing the gospel to an enormous, captive audience watching my documentary.

It seemed to me that God's hand was in the process from the beginning, as miracle after miracle took place. We had a renowned mustang trainer who looked like we plucked him straight from a Wrangler jeans commercial and four young men whose stories and personalities were perfect for the narrative of taming wild mustangs. And of course, the setting was incredible: a ranch in a valley surrounded by fourteen-thousand-foot mountain peaks. Plus millions of dollars in funding to make it all happen. Soon, we were heading to Colorado to begin the program.

Within the first couple of weeks at the ranch, it was clear that I was no longer the star of the show. In fact, I was never the star of the show—not to anyone outside of my own mind. Grant's one-liners and ability to apply the gospel in unique circumstances captivated everyone who watched the training sessions. The four participants and their broken yet redeemable stories grabbed the hearts of all who knew them.

Me, on the other hand? I pretty much only showed up when things were going wrong. Oftentimes, I was the one throwing gas on the fire, stumbling my way through mentoring four severely at-risk young men in ways I was not fully equipped to do.

One day, I pulled my teammates Micah and Kelsey into the office and broke into tears. “This is not what I envisioned whatsoever. I did not come here to just train horses. This is so much bigger than that!” I think they were a little taken aback by how emphatic I was. As much as I had a point that the rehabilitation program was bigger than horse training, I tried my best to hide the real reason why I was upset: I wasn’t getting the recognition I wanted. I had envisioned myself as the hero who would take these young men on a life-changing journey with my wisdom and heart-transforming affirmations. I wanted them to see their need for Jesus, become sold-out followers of him, and have a testimony that would awe anyone who heard it. But I wanted to be the main character in their testimony, and I felt like my glory was being robbed.

The training was going brilliantly. The boys were growing spiritually. But I was not the star.

Kelsey gently pulled me aside a few days after my outburst. “Ryan, if you start to make this about you, the Lord will take it from you.” I heard her words, but like James and John, I had no real grasp of what Jesus meant when he asked if they would be willing to suffer. I had no idea how true those words would be. I continued to fumble my way through a long two months, doing my best to help these boys, yet failing. All of my mistakes and the dumb things I seemed to say at every turn were immortalized on film for the rest of my life.

When our time at the ranch was almost over, and I realized how bad I looked in real time, I wanted to do some "image management." I believed that I needed to craft a narrative and a brand around myself to see the mustang rehabilitation program succeed. And I only had a little bit of time to do it. I spoke with multiple marketing experts who told me, "Build your brand! Boost your social media presence! Increase the public awareness about Ryan Miller!"

The experts who encouraged me to lean heavily into the idea of "building a brand" weren't doing anything new. Brands are all the rage. They are the commodification of personalities and identities. They help us connect with who or what we give our time and attention to. Brands are easy to identify, to spot from afar, and to understand. And if you are marketing something—especially yourself—you want to be all those things: easy to find, understandable, and fascinating to look at.

But our modern ideas about branding miss the dangerous implications. "Branding" is a process that originated on ranches and farmlands, something that was pragmatic in nature. And not only that, but a brand was painful. Writer Dan Braga tells about his experience watching the branding process: "I've stood on the rails of a squeeze chute, watching. . . . The cow gets locked in a head gate, the iron is applied, and it jolts from the initial pain, sometimes letting out a shocked 'moo.' The smell of burning hair fills the air as the cow is released, now marked with its owner's brand for life. A brand is a burn scar."[8]

Branding something means to mark ownership. And that mark tells everyone who sees it that the one who bears it belongs to someone else.

When you think about it, a brand is the same thing for us today: an indicator of who owns us. Too often, it's our own self-image.

What the marketing experts were telling me about building my personal brand was, essentially, "You need to become an influencer, Ryan." Those words washed over me like a warm bath on a frigid day. It was everything I wanted. Sharing the gospel to a waiting audience made sense. This was how the world worked. Marketing was about creating buzz on social media platforms, and the way to do that was to gain influence and a large following. So clearly, if we were going to build a movement, we needed someone at the forefront pushing the message, and not only was I happy to step up to the plate, but it was an itch I desperately wanted scratched.

And then my wife spoke up.

"Why do you want to become an influencer?" she asked.

"Well, it's not that I want it. It's just what's best for the project."

I could see her looking at me with questions in her eyes, as if she could see right through my words and into my motives.

"But, *why*, Ryan? You say you don't 'want' it, but do you think, honestly, that's the path God has you on? I'm not saying it isn't. I just think we need to pray for more clarity before jumping in head first," she said.

Instead of leaning in humbly to her questions, I felt myself getting angry. "Are you suggesting I would be doing this for prideful gain? How can you say that? You're my wife. You know me better than that! And this is just what's necessary!" I lashed out at her, all the while knowing deep down that I had been found out. She *did* know me better than that. I was basically gaslighting the person I love most in the world in order to defend my pride.

Looking back now, I can see that my behavior modeled that of an addict lashing out when his drug of choice is being threatened. I didn't know at the time that my whole life I had been medicating with the drug of acclaim—and it's a dangerous drug, because we can disguise it as innocent, even godly. Here, I had the rare chance to get higher than I'd ever been before, and I wasn't going to let anyone get in the way—even my wife.

Here is the strange thing about this high: I still believe it was coupled with pure intentions and a desire to serve the Lord. Now, you might think that can't be true, but it was. I had convinced myself that increasing my personal popularity was a necessary part of growing the brand and creating more buzz around the rehabilitation program. All of this was so the gospel could reach more people. My mindset had become "I must increase, so he can also increase."

That is not what Scripture says. But as embarrassing as it is to confess my mindset, to put these words on a page, I don't think I'm alone. This mindset has crept into and consumed much of the American church.

THE GIFT OF OBSCURITY

I have many friends from college who have become pastors. I've had the chance to speak at various churches over the years. And I have seen the level of fear that many churches operate under. It's like a magnet slowly pulling the leadership of the church inch by inch closer to how our current culture would define what "success" is. As fear of irrelevance leads the way, much of the shocking message of Jesus has been traded for another. "Lose your life to find it" has been traded for "You can have it all because you're blessed and highly favored in the Lord." We seem to have lost our true north of the pure and simple gospel, looking instead to the right and to the left for the cool breeze of affirmation, grasping after the winds of "finally arriving."

For many pastors I've spoken with, the thing that keeps them up at night is weekly attendance and tithing totals—metrics that are closely tied to success in staying culturally relevant from the pulpit. It makes sense. Without people, there is no church. And without the money those churchgoers bring, the lights in the building can't stay on. But often, if you follow the deepest fear of the leader of any organization, you will find the true north of the organization. Dare I say, too many churches are driven by the fear of becoming obsolete, small, insignificant. So the response is to follow what will keep people in the seats.

I love the church. I know many great pastors with big, selfless hearts. I don't want to leave you with the impression that there is no good in the church. I've seen pastors and leaders labor over sermons and humbly beg the Lord in prayer for his Spirit to do what they cannot in the hearts of listeners as they preach.

But there is a risk to the way we have structured churches. We tend to revere, or even worship, the leaders we love—and many leaders don't hate that. As a leader, I have to fight that temptation every single day. The stage, a place of prominence, is the most dangerous place a Christian like me can be. I'm telling you this as someone who is a social media influencer and has chased the spotlight my whole life, and I'm preaching to myself as I write these words: In a culture clamoring to be known, God often calls his people to hiddenness.

As I look back on my life, I see that my greatest times of joy have come during seasons of obscurity. On the flip side, my greatest times of want and unrest have come when I have clamored to be seen.

Years ago, I had the chance to speak at a Cru conference to a few thousand high school students. I thought I killed it. I spoke with passion and purpose and shared some pretty convincing words about God to all of the eager ears in the audience. I stepped off the stage feeling good—and valuable.

My mentor, Connor, was the president of the Cru high school ministry at the time. He had heard my message, and not long after I stepped off the stage, he approached me with some feedback.

"Ryan," he said, "I have to be honest, it felt like you were on your toes the whole time you were on stage. You were trying so hard to reach the kids, but your flesh was showing much more than the Spirit. Your eagerness seemed to be about impressing the students, not about making God look impressive. And I have to tell you, as I was watching you and praying for you, I felt like the Lord said, 'Ryan needs to go burrow under a mountain. He needs to go into a season where no one sees him. It's not going to be easy for him, but he will come out refined if he does.'"

As with many of the most important lessons in my life, it took me a long time to understand the depth and necessity of what Connor was telling me. The Lord was going to force me into a season of hiddenness whether I wanted it or not, but he knew that's where I had to be.

A mustang is wild, and that's a good thing. But a mustang must also endure the round pen to be tamed. And a man or woman of God must also burrow under the mountain. Both realities are sacred and necessary. Our growth and the impact of any work we do is only going to be as high as the roots are deep.

And the roots only grow strong in obscurity.

MEEK MOMENT

If you want to pursue meekness and grow spiritual roots, begin by asking God to direct you. You can start by praying this prayer:

> *Lord Jesus, stir the affections, the passions, and the wildness in my heart and redirect them toward*

you and your Kingdom. Let the ownership of my life be firmly placed in your hands. Mark me for your name, not the world's. Don't let me chase after building a brand, but rather build a foundation of love in you.

Help me to see that the greatest gift I could ever have in this life is not a stage or a platform but a bit in my mouth and a saddle on my back. I want to witness the upside-down Kingdom of God—and the adventure that comes with it. Allow me to see the promotion that comes through hiddenness, to feel your presence in the wilderness, and to know that every season of obscurity is formative—it's you shaping me into your warhorse.

Amen.

THE HEALTH OF YOUR SOUL

In Mark 1:21-38, the disciple Mark opens his exposition of Jesus' ministry by showing how quickly Jesus grew in popularity as he preached the gospel and healed many people. We see that "[the people] were astonished at his teaching" and "at once his fame spread everywhere throughout all the surrounding region of Galilee."[9] It's the dream of so many pastors, writers, and content creators, isn't it? To "go viral." To break onto the scene with our projects, our can't-look-away videos, our sermons—and immediately have hundreds of thousands of downloads, Amazon reviews, and new followers clamoring for more. No one is immune to the dopamine hit of those tiny red notifications throwing affirmation our way.

Mark goes on to describe how "the whole city was gathered together at the door" as Jesus healed many who were sick and drove out the demons who tormented others.[10] Can you imagine the scene? The jostling for position in line, the whispers of "There he is; it's Jesus of Nazareth; I see him!" A Hollywood red carpet has nothing on the demand for the man who could actually heal people of the illnesses and evil spirits that had devastated them for years.

And yet the very next morning, at the height of Jesus' popularity in that region, when there were hundreds, perhaps thousands, of people lining up to see and hear more from him, Jesus was nowhere to be found. He had gone to a desolate place to pray to his Father.[11]

So Peter went looking for Jesus. We can imagine his bewilderment at why Jesus would leave town right as his ministry was growing and gaining credibility and attention, because we would wonder the same today. "Everyone is looking for you," Peter told Jesus.[12]

"You're growing in popularity; you need to get back down there and do something, Jesus," Peter implied with his words, echoing sentiments we've all heard or said to others. Certainly this was what the marketing experts were pushing me to do: "You've got the Internet's attention for a moment, so capitalize! All press is good press. Here's your chance to keep building your platform!"

Jesus' response to Peter? He got up, and he left. He modeled the meekness of someone whose eyes were not on himself or his ministry but on obeying the Father's will. "Let us go on to the next towns, that I may preach there also, for *that is why* I came out," he said.[13] It wasn't that Jesus didn't care about the people waiting to see him. It was that he was confident that he did what he came to do: preach the gospel of repentance and faith. And he would continue to preach that word until everyone had heard it. He understood that popularity is fleeting, a hamster wheel of performance and entertainment to keep the lines of people coming. But the work Jesus came to do is the opposite of fleeting. The message of the gospel will remain. It will speak for itself much longer than the attention span of the masses.

Author and pastor Zack Eswine beautifully sums up the pull to be seen and acclaimed when he writes, "As you enter ministry, you will be tempted to orient your desires toward doing large things in famous ways as fast and as efficiently as you can. But. . . . Almost anything in life that truly matters will require you to do small, mostly overlooked things, over a long period of time with [Jesus]."[14]

In this Internet and social media age, it's easy for leaders and creators of all types to imagine ourselves as the exception to the model that has been set before us. We can be tempted to put the word "gospel" on any ambition and believe it deserves to be blessed and popular.

Jesus' life and ministry show us what Kingdom work really looks like: fiercely guarding our souls and our fellowship with

God, prioritizing time in a desolate place with our Father, and committing ourselves to diligence in the work itself. Most of us will never be known, much less remembered, for more than a moment. But if our lives and our work are an overflow of his presence and fellowship, they will matter exactly where they are supposed to matter the most: right where we are.

CHAPTER 6

YOUR FEAR IS ACTUALLY YOUR PRIDE

Thus says the LORD: "Let not the wise man boast in his wisdom, let not the mighty man boast in his might, let not the rich man boast in his riches, but let him who boasts boast in this, that he understands and knows me."

JEREMIAH 9:23-24, ESV

I started writing this book nearly a decade ago, when I was twenty-six years old. One of the first things I wrote about was Moses' rejection of God's assignment for him to return to Egypt and lead his people, the Israelites, out of slavery.[1] I went on and on about Moses' fear, citing how many times he asked God to send someone else because he was sure that the Lord had the wrong guy. My takeaway was that we should not be like Moses but rather have the courage to trust God at his first ask, to step immediately into obedience without delay.

It's a good thing God made me wait so long to write *this* version instead. Because in the middle of writing about meekness, God exposed my own misunderstanding of the virtue. For the sake of making a bold point, I had called into question a hero of the faith for doubting what God could do through someone like him. In reality—knowing the whole arc and story of his life—Moses could likely be described as one of the meekest men to ever walk the planet.

It's hard for us today to understand the scale of what God was asking Moses to do. The Israelites had been in slavery in Egypt for upward of four hundred years, so we are talking about several generations born, raised, and dying in slavery. In Exodus 3, God says to Moses, "I have indeed seen the misery of my people in Egypt. I have heard them crying out because of their slave drivers, and I am concerned about their suffering. So I have come down to rescue them from the hand of the Egyptians. . . . So now, go. I am sending you to Pharaoh to bring my people the Israelites out of Egypt."[2]

Are you kidding?! Just waltz right into the palace of the most powerful man in the ancient world and tell him to let hundreds of thousands of people—all of the country's free labor, the economic legs of the entire social structure of Egypt—walk out on their jobs, or else? It would be like someone with a criminal record, who not only had filthy feet and unkempt hair but who also held absolutely no political capital or influence, walking into the White House and demanding that the president of the United States dismantle the military. He would be laughed out of the building. And Moses knew he would be too. The task God had put before him was so grand, so impossible, that *of course* Moses couldn't wrap his head around it! Moses was an anointed man, but he was still a man, full of sin, with a heart prone to rage. His reaction to the Lord's plan for his life was real and honest, but I mistook it for cowardice because I wanted him to walk up to Pharaoh with swagger.

I couldn't see with my privileged American eyes the enormity of what Moses was being asked to do.

Here was Moses, having fled from the most powerful country in the world, from the most powerful man in the world, because of his crime of murder. After Moses lived among sheep for forty years, God asked him to return to the country that had hated him to ask their leader to hand over their most valuable commodity: their Hebrew slaves.

Like me, maybe you read these stories in the Bible without understanding just how grand these acts of courageous faithfulness really were. We've become so accustomed to comfort that it has hurt our ability to grasp the level of boldness these men and women of the Bible had. Sure, we believe the Bible's stories are true, but they have become partially mythologized to the point that it's hard to read them as what they are: historical nonfiction. The events in the Bible actually happened! Yet, we can be quick to look for the application of these stories to our own lives, thinking we are the Moses or the Esther of the story, putting ourselves in the center of the narrative. The awe that should serve to increase our faith becomes a ho-hum sentiment, a nursery rhyme for grown-ups.

When we read the Bible like that, we miss the whole point. That's exactly what I was doing ten years ago. With that posture, I was not ready to understand all that was standing between me and growing in meekness.

SUPER WHAT?

After the rehabilitation program had wrapped up and I was rebuilding my work life, longing to walk in God's will, I had the idea to start a nonprofit focused on mental health. I had hoped that after people watched the transformation of the boys on the ranch, they would be inspired to change their own lives. I felt responsible to create resources that could help, or at the very least be a starting place, and that's when Share the Struggle, the nonprofit, was born. My buddy Reid, a laid-back, surfer-type dude who abides with the Lord in ways I definitely didn't at that point in time, came on board as the operator of the organization to be the antidote to all of my intensity. God was still dealing with me pretty severely in terms of my pride. Coming off the season of filming and directing a documentary had revealed some pretty gross truths about my heart. For much of the time on the ranch, I wanted to be the hero. I obsessed over how I was being portrayed and what people would think of me. Truthfully, I saw myself look bad in a lot of situations.

But because of that experience, I was trying to be a different man moving forward. As Reid and I started to build Share the Struggle, it should not have surprised me that God would find plenty of opportunities to keep sanctifying me.

One afternoon, Reid called. After some small talk, he said, "Ryan, I was praying for you this morning, and the Lord gave me a vision about you."

"Okay, man, cool," I responded. I don't often get calls like this, and whenever I hear someone say they heard from the Lord without a good amount of Scripture attached, I tend to be skeptical. But I trusted Reid and his relationship with Jesus. Working closely with him, I had come to find Reid to be one of the wisest, most humble, and most prayerful dudes I'd ever met. So when he said he had a vision for me, I knew I should listen. I was excited, hoping Reid was about to share some sort of future prosperous and popular version of my life with me. "Tell me about it!" I encouraged him.

"Well, I've been pretty hesitant to, actually." He started listing disclaimers before he said any more.

My enthusiasm faded, along with the smile of anticipation on my face. I was nodding my head against the phone, waiting, thinking, *Okay, give it to me, bro.*

And then he did: "I don't mean for this to be offensive, but I feel like I need to share. In the vision, I saw you standing before this big city, and in front of everyone, you grew and inflated into this chisel-jawed, superhero-looking man. You put your hands on your hips, classic Superman style, and for a minute you were standing there tall and proud. And as I was seeing it, I thought it made a lot of sense. You know, *Ryan is stepping into uncharted territory, taking risks, charging the hill for the Kingdom*. I thought, *Ryan is the guy God is going to use to save people; he's going to do big things. He's the right one to lead this new nonprofit and to spearhead this mission to help believers in their deepest mental health struggles*."

Oh, I thought to myself. *Well, I don't hate where this is going.*

But then Reid gave more disclaimers about the rest of

what he saw, as if he was preparing me for a heavy blow. Finally, I said, "Dude, just tell me!"

"I saw you deflate, Ryan. Like the plug was pulled on you, air came out of your superhero body, and in front of everyone in this big city, you melted into one of those wacky inflatable figures that we see at used-car dealerships."

Ohhhh.

"And then," Reid took a breath to pause before he said, "it became clear what the Lord was saying: 'This is what Ryan looks like in the Kingdom when he elevates himself.'"

Now at this point in my life, I was hungry for meekness. I didn't want to be the guy who read the Bible and saw the flaws in others while ignoring the flaws in myself. I truly craved meekness—to be bold for the Kingdom while surrendering fully to the Lord—and I wanted more of Jesus. God had put me in the right place to receive this kind of feedback from someone I trusted. When I told Reid, "Thank you," I meant it. I held on to that image to remind myself of who I am, and who God is. *When you elevate yourself, you'll be humbled; when you humble yourself, you'll be elevated.*[3]

PRIDE'S MASK

Around the time that Reid shared his vision, it began to feel like everything around me was crumbling. It was one of those seasons in life where nothing falls into place, and the things that I'd looked forward to happening seemed to vanish into thin air.

I started having panic attacks for the first time in my life, where my muscles tightened up and my chest felt so heavy I could hardly breath. Anxiety and fear bubbled up in me the moment I woke up, and I dreaded the day ahead. I felt like someone was out to get me, something was going to go wrong, and my life and ministry were about to fall apart right before my eyes.

I called one of my mentors, Connor, to process all I was feeling. Connor is the wisest person I know and one of those guys who seems to have a direct line to Jesus when he prays. I broke down for Connor all the irons I had in the fire, how hard I was working, and how essential each of my responsibilities were. I told him about the low-grade anxiety I felt throughout the day, the looming feeling that something bad was going to happen, and the general dissatisfaction that underscored almost every part of my life. I went on and on for a good thirty minutes, sharing all the emotions and circumstances before I finally stopped talking and waited for his response.

Connor took a thoughtful moment to gather himself, and then he began, "Well, man, this might be hard to hear, but . . ."

Oh great, I thought to myself. *Here we go again—more correction.*

"Ryan," Connor continued, "I think your pride is masking itself as fear."

Now that's a sentence that hit me hard, especially coming from someone with the relational capital in my life to say it with authority.

At first, I inwardly scoffed a bit, feeling defensive and trying to piece together how that was even possible. I did not at all feel like the problem was that I thought too highly of myself. At that point in time, in the wake of a humiliating experience with the mustang program, I had a pretty low view of myself. And then Reid had shared the wacky inflatable-man vision, and I couldn't get that out of my head either. I hung up my call with Connor even more discouraged. *Wow*, I thought. *Even in my weakest, most broken moments, I'm still being told that I'm a prideful punk.*

In my head, I was in a humble place. How could feeling on the verge of panic be prideful? How could an out-of-control, weak, can't-breathe-tight-chest type of existence really be pride? The wacky, inflatable, arm-flailing tube man trying to be Superman? *That* was for sure pride. But panic attacks? I was more confused than ever.

MEEK MOMENT

If you're feeling anxious today, take a moment to breathe and pause here. Get a piece of paper and write down three things you're afraid of. It could be fears about parenting, money, jobs, relationships, failures. I call this fear-storming. The goal is to get the worries out of your head and onto paper. Name them, because doing so helps the fear feel smaller right away.

Now I want you to visualize placing each of those fears onto a saddle in front of you. The Bible tells us to cast our cares on him, for he cares for us.[4] Casting is not a dainty motion, but one that takes effort, rhythm, strength, and a lot of practice. Think of it like lifting a saddle onto a horse. You have to learn the movement, feel the weight of the saddle you're holding, stop fighting the heaviness of it, and start trusting the momentum of the swing. That takes a lot of reps.

So give it your first rep right now. Imagine the weight of your fears being heaved onto the saddle. Picture them on the back of a horse, as you let someone stronger than you hold the weight. Because that's who God is: the one who carries what you cannot.

Now, I want to be clear: Anxiety manifests itself differently in all of us. There are genetic, biological forms of generalized anxiety disorder that cause people innumerable kinds of physical distress. Right now, I know there are people of all ages, races, genders, and socioeconomic statuses up all night, tossing and turning, unable to control the intrusive thoughts in their brains because of wild rushes of stress hormones that cannot be turned off. Anxiety does not discriminate. There are chemical conditions that require treatment, and we should rightly see advanced medical knowledge for mental health concerns as a grace from the Lord.

I have seen in others and experienced in myself the kind of anxiety that begins somewhere outside our control. But I also know that much, maybe even most, of the anxiety in my own life started somewhere within my control. That's what I want to address here.

ANXIOUS MESSES

After I was given the vision of the wacky, inflatable, arm-flailing tube man from Reid and the startling message about pride from Connor, I needed about a year to fully understand how far the cultural current of self-worship had swept me away into a mindset of fear. I was not a victim of the amount of work I had on my plate, unfair treatment, or the weight of my responsibilities. I was guilty of making my world about myself. And my pride had begun to manifest itself as fear, worry, and anxiety.

I understand the sensitive nature of the topic of anxiety. When you are struggling with stress or general anxiety, it's difficult to hear that you are responsible to do something about it. I've been there. But as hard as it might be to face the truth, it needs to be wrestled with because the Bible could not be clearer: Jesus commands us not to be anxious, and excessive worry can sometimes lead to a lack of faith in or disobedience to God.[5] It keeps us from the good work God has in store for our lives. But take heart, because while *all* of us are, in some measure, anxious people, God has given us the promise of peace.

There is a difference between biological anxiety disorders and the kind of stress that results from spinning yourself to the ground in hustle culture, but *both* can be offered up in prayer. Anxiety in any form can be taken before the Lord in faith, even if there isn't an easy fix. Vulnerably bringing our worries to him can become the joy of our lives, because healing takes place at the cross where we truly lose our lives, see the love of God poured out for us, and become completely undone in that love.

My concern is that we have become so swept away in the cultural current of self that we can no longer see our pride as it is and grasp the implications of taking up our cross, losing our lives, and being crucified with Christ. That's the state I was in before Connor identified my pride for what it was. A sad result of my self-focus and unwillingness to die to myself was a life out of order. And this life out of order gave birth to fear and worry.

It might seem offensive to suggest to someone experiencing stress, fear, or worry that pride could be the root. Talk about adding insult to injury, kicking someone when they are already down. That's how I felt after my conversation with Connor. But we can't bury our heads in the sand when it comes to these realities. And my hunch is that for a lot of you reading this, when you allow yourself to be honest, the idea that pride could be masking itself as fear hits home. But there is an antidote found in Jesus and available to all of us: meekness.

THE MEEKNESS ANTIDOTE

The thing about meekness is that nobody can ever truly see the meekness in someone else's heart, or even their own heart. It's not like you can outdo someone else in showing meekness. It just doesn't make sense. But we can, in an effort to have more meekness, learn how to spot false meekness in ourselves. In those moments after talking to Reid and Connor about my pride, I was a basket case of self-loathing, letting toxic negative thoughts run wild in my mind and thinking lowly of myself. The way I spoke changed. I had less energy. And I pawned it off as being "wounded" or "burned out" or "recovering."

Now, with a little perspective, I *can* see that my pride was masking itself as fear and my humility was as counterfeit as it comes. I had yet to realize that this type of fabricated meekness was in my heart until it was called out on me. All I did after being on the wacky-inflatable-arm-flailing-Superman side of the pendulum was swing over to the other side, all the while missing the true meekness Jesus had for me outside of my self-focus.

Just as federal agents study real money in order to better identify what is counterfeit, I knew it was vital for me to see what real humility was so I could spot the fake version in myself. Let's face it—when it comes to humility in the Christian community, we can be master manipulators. We like outward appearances to be nice and neat, to be seen as gentle "Oh bless your heart" kind of people. But that's not the life we're called to.

Jesus tells us that the call on a believer's life is to pick up our cross, die to ourselves, and be willing to lose it all for his name's sake. And when we die to ourselves, we don't become more polite; we become more obedient, convicted, and bold than ever before. In the Bible, we rarely see the apostles pray for physical safety and security. In fact, they often prayed to the Lord for more boldness.[6] I wonder, if we took inventory of the church's prayers, or even of our own, what percentage would go to praying for more boldness as opposed to safe travels and blessings for our food?

What if we flipped our thinking and identified when our fear is actually pride and self-preoccupation? What if we embraced meekness instead, choosing a life of self-denial and sacrifice? What if we were bold enough to go against what's popular in our society and culture? Jesus was clear that if we follow him, we need to prepare to be hated.[7] That if the world persecuted him, they would persecute us as well. Even so, if we are truly pursuing meekness, one of the first things to fall away should be the opinions of the world. The warhorse running into battle isn't concerned about the noise of the onlookers—only the master on his back, guiding him where he needs to go.

MEEK MOMENT

If you want to embrace meekness and start letting God take control, you can start by praying this prayer.

> *Lord, we know that when we cast our cares on you, something beautiful happens: Our once restless, anxious, and wild hearts become steady under your hand. The fears that once ruled us become saddles that you carry, and the reins that*

turned our knuckles white from gripping rest safely in your hands. Father, we know that peace is one of the greatest gifts of a meek life, so we ask for your peace to settle into the places in our lives where anxiety has taken up residence for too long.

Amen.

THE PURSUIT OF A LIFETIME

I confessed where I was at spiritually as a twenty-six-year-old guy, when I first thought, *Maybe God wants me to write a book about meekness.* And while I hope I have grown in holiness in the last decade, one thing I can tell you for sure is that I am much more aware of my sin than twenty-six-year-old Ryan was. It's not lost on me how desperately I need Jesus on this side of eternity. Because even now, in this season while I write *this* book, the one you hold in your hands, I'm still confusing my pride with my fear.

I have a bad habit of taking on more and more work, feeling like I have to be more efficient, produce more content, and *Hustle! Hustle! Hustle!* to the point that I start flailing and comparing myself to other content creators who are reaching more people. Once I get in that comparison trap, I feel crappy that objectively, by the numbers, I'm not as good as them. My business coach said, "I think you're afraid of future failure, so you spin yourself into chaos to try to prevent living out your fear, which is, at the root, that you're not good enough, that you don't stack up. To fight your fear, you do more and more things."

I knew he was right. That's my default mode: pile on the work and try to be great. I responded, "I think the reason I do so much is because I don't want to be known as just another influencer. It's stupid, I know, but if that is all I'm known as, it's clear I'm not the best. There are other people doing this work who are better than me. And when I see that, then I *know* I'm not enough. If I keep giving myself other titles, like filmmaker, business owner, nonprofit executive, all this other stuff that I'm doing, I have an excuse to not be as good as the next influencer. Even saying it out loud, I know how it sounds. Fear that is really pride. But that's where my thoughts go."

Recently, a friend of mine had a vision of me. There was a calendar with pages that were turning really fast, like a flip book, and not stopping. Then my friend heard the Lord say, "Stop and smell the roses, Ryan. You're not enjoying what is right around you. You're missing time, and you're missing the process of growth I'm putting you through. You're frantic." It sounds a lot like a wacky inflatable man in front of a used-car dealership.

NOTHING TO LOSE

Maybe the most influential hero of the faith to me is Jim Elliot. After reading about his life in his journals from when he was a college student, I decided I wanted to live like him.

Jim was a wild man! He was a wrestler at Wheaton College, was a jokester, and got in his fair share of trouble. But he was also devoted and in love with the Lord. As a college freshman, he wrote with the conviction of a martyr, so it's not surprising that he eventually became one. Years later, Jim, with his wife, Elisabeth, and a few other couples from Wheaton, went down to Ecuador to share the gospel with an unreached tribe, the Waorani. This tribe was given the name *Auca*, which means "savage," by a neighboring tribe, because anyone who tried to make contact with them was killed. Oil and logging companies and other explorers were all driven away, if not murdered, by the Waorani. Many people advised the couples not to go, even calling them crazy for it.

But these five men, led by Jim Elliot, didn't care. They knew they had marching orders to reach this tribe, so they obeyed the Lord and went amid the backlash from many people. For a while, they flew their plane over the tribe's land, dropping gifts and food. They wanted to make friends and show that they were simply there to help. Eventually, they felt that it was time to make contact with the tribe. The men stepped off the plane and were greeted by a few curious Waorani women, followed by a man from the tribe.

Back at their temporary homes in the jungle, the missionaries' wives waited patiently for news, praying that God would protect the men as they entered hostile territory. But hours of waiting turned into days, and slowly they began to face the reality that their husbands had likely been killed and would not be returning. The bodies of four of the men were found three days later down the river, with spears through their chests. The fifth was never recovered.

It would be easy to call their mission a hopeless failure. When word got back to the United States and the rest of the world, many saw the situation as nothing more than a devastating moment. Five innocent lives taken from their families. And for what?

Eventually it came out that the five men all had guns on them but never used them. Some years later, Elisabeth Elliot and the other wives returned to Ecuador. A Waorani girl named Dayuma taught these women the local language, and when the Lord told them to go back to the very people who had killed their husbands and share the gospel with them, they did. The entire tribe came to know Jesus as their Savior.[8]

Jim Elliot's journals were later shared with the world, and in them he penned words that give us a glimpse into the heart of a man willing to lose everything. He inspired millions of believers around the world with this resonant truth: "He is no fool who gives what he cannot keep to gain what he cannot lose." Elliot and his friends were not swayed one bit by others' words and didn't even pull their guns when they were approached with the spears of the Waorani fighters. They were built out of the iron of pure conviction and resolve—all which came from brokenhearted boldness and fearless surrender.

A mustang who has given all their freedom, autonomy, and power in service of their master has in fact gained more of all of those things. God chooses the mustang-like among us for bold purposes because we understand this trade-off. A wild mustang doesn't start with anything. In fact, he is branded and discarded to life in a cage because his hardened exterior, forged by a life of adversity, looks more like a liability. And left alone, that kind of reckless wild can be exactly that—a liability.

But a wild spirit who has nothing to lose but everything to gain? That is the rare person who lays down all their pride, submits to the Lord, willingly picks up their cross, follows his lead, and says, "Your will, not mine." It is the mustang spirit that Jesus was looking for in his followers. Because when you have lost everything but a cause to fight for and someone to serve, you're not even thinking about yourself enough to feel fear, and you really do have everything to gain.

CHAPTER 7

THE GRACE OF THE WILDERNESS

The LORD is good to those who wait for him, to the soul who seeks him.

LAMENTATIONS 3:25, ESV

If there is one thing that we are almost universally not good at, it's waiting. We get frustrated at stoplights, irritable in drive-through lines that take more than a few minutes, and annoyed at web pages that take more than eight seconds to load.[1] Eight seconds, and our capacity to wait is maxed out.

The problem is, God is never in the kind of hurry we are. The pace at which we make plans and set out to accomplish great things and check items off our to-do lists is rarely the pace at which God moves.

Our God is a God who waits, and we are not people who know how to wait very well.

But learning meekness and living with the kind of selflessness required of a meek man or woman will, without a doubt, require us to wait. When I first began to dive into the subject of meekness, I started to see that in Scripture, meekness and waiting are held closely together. Colossians 3:12 says, "Put on then, as God's chosen ones, holy and beloved, compassionate hearts, kindness, humility, *meekness, and patience*."[2] Sentiments like this are all over the New Testament. These two character traits are nearly inseparable, and it really makes perfect sense. Because the heroes of God from the Bible—people who embodied what it means to be meek—almost without exception had to endure seasons of waiting before becoming instruments in God's master plan.

Abraham and Sarah waited twenty-five years from the time God promised them a son to the day of his birth. They did not exactly wait well and have faith in that promise, but that's another story.

Jacob waited fourteen years for his love, Rachel, to become his wife.

Joseph was forced to work in slavery and wait in prison for thirteen years before he was given a new position of influence in the Egyptian government.

The Israelites waited four hundred years in slavery in Egypt. Then Moses spent another forty years leading them in the wilderness before reaching the land the Lord had promised to give them.

Elijah waited for rain.

Hannah waited for a baby.

David waited for years after his anointing, many of them spent running for his life, to become the king of Israel.

Waiting is one of God's greatest means of sanctification, of making us a little more like him. Waiting reveals so much about us: our true motives, our first loves, even the things we idolize that capture our affections more than the heart of God.

Waiting forces us into a posture of surrender as it reveals how little we really control about our lives. Seasons of longing for "the next thing" drive us to the reality that whatever it is we want so badly, it's actually not ours. Everything we have is from the Lord, and we don't get to demand when we are given anything.

But while waiting forces us to surrender all that we want most, it also *replaces* what we want most.

LIKE KIDS ON A ROAD TRIP

One of the greatest examples of this kind of waiting is the life of Moses, who had to endure not only wandering through the desert but the constant questioning and complaining of the Israelites. How many times did they say to him, "Why did you bring us up out of Egypt?"[3] And how many more times than are even recorded in Scripture must Moses have looked to God to ask, "What should I do with these people?"[4]

While most of us can't relate to wandering in the desert for decades, we've all experienced the complaints that come from waiting. I imagine being on a road trip with my kids and every few minutes hearing "Are we there yet?" "I'm hungry!" "I'm bored." "I want to go home." Even though I've told them,

"But we are going to the ocean, and it's amazing! We will build sandcastles and jump in the waves and look for dolphins and eat snow cones on the boardwalk! We just have to get through this road trip. We have to wait patiently until we get there." In a child's mind, the promise of the ocean is not greater than the angst of the car ride, and the waiting feels unbearable.

We are all like children on a road trip. Or Israelites in the wilderness.

When Moses led the Israelites out of Egypt, they didn't know where they were going or how long their journey would be—only that there was a land promised to them and that God would take them there. They were told that milk and honey would be flowing sometime in the unknown future, but each morning they woke up to only a daily supply of manna.* Every night they went to sleep wondering if the next day would be their first in the new home they had heard such wonderful things about. This journey might not sound all that difficult, because yes, they had miraculous manna from heaven. But think about living this way day in and day out for forty years, in the barren, hot desert. It would be utterly exhausting. There was also constant warfare with surrounding nations, fighting with fellow Israelites, and an ever-present possibility of all manner of threats lurking around the corner. Any of us would get grumpy, and it's safe to say most of us would start to have doubts about who was leading us and where he was planning to go.

* See Exodus 16. Manna was the daily food God provided for the Israelites in the desert for forty years.

There's no other way to put it—the wilderness sucks. Waiting isn't fun. It feels like the enemy.

But it's actually a true friend, because God does some of his best work in the wilderness.

MEEK MOMENT

There's something so beautiful about going through the wilderness or walking through a season of real hardship, because after it's over, you stop fearing whatever it was you had to go through. You've already faced it. With the help of the Lord and his sustaining presence, you've made it through whatever it was that worried you.

Intrusive thoughts are often just what-if thoughts.

What if I lose my job?

What if they don't like me?

What if my finances collapse?

What if my kids don't follow Jesus?

But Philippians 4:6–8 makes it clear—we're not just called to get rid of our what-if thoughts. We're called to replace them with what-is affirmations. Replace your troubled thoughts with the truth today. *I am called, loved, chosen, cared for. I am made in the image of a good God. I don't need to fear.*

THE DEATH OF A DREAM

When our time at the ranch was coming to an end, I was ready to take the next step. In my mind, that meant making a documentary about my experience taming mustangs—and wild lives. But as we started the process, dozens of small tech issues, most of which could be resolved, kept slowing things down. Emails never got to the right person or somehow were never received. It was not one fatal blow but a hundred little paper cuts.

Finally, one day my wife, Annie, was sitting across from me on the couch. As we were talking, she stopped, looked right at me, and said, "Whoa. I had a vision." Now, this is not typical of Annie. She's so measured, and she's not usually a woman who will stop in the middle of a sentence to share a vision. But as Annie held my eye contact, she continued, "Ryan, I had a vision of your project in a tomb."

Um, that's not good. I already had low-grade anxiety about the project, and now my wife's fears had brought back to the surface all that I had been pushing down for quite some time. Because yeah, weird stuff was happening, but I felt like we were on our way. We hadn't finished the project yet, but that was still the plan.

At this point in my life, I started hearing from the Lord in new ways. Before then, my communion with God had mostly come through spending time in Scripture. I would still say that is one of the most important means of hearing from God. But in this season, God was beginning to show himself to me in other ways, especially through pictures and images that I knew could only be from him. The week after my wife told me what she had seen, I woke up to my own image of the project. It was, this time, in a coffin. The picture is still vivid to me: a maroon, velvet-lined coffin. Two clear warnings, back-to-back. In hindsight, I should have gotten out of bed and immediately canceled everything.

But I didn't. I wasn't ready to accept the death of this dream. Instead, I didn't tell anyone what I had seen, because I hoped this was all in my head. I didn't tell Annie, and I definitely didn't tell my teammate Kelsey because the next day we had an online meeting with our agents.

Early in this meeting, as discussions were ramping up to the next step and we were given hypothetical scenarios to consider, Kelsey interrupted the call and asked, "Guys, can I talk to Ryan offline for a few minutes before we go any further?"

Our team looked at us through the screen with quizzical and slightly concerned faces, but one of them piped up and answered, "Yes, of course. We will circle back soon."

Kelsey and I hopped on another call, and through a slightly shaky voice, she said, "I'm so hesitant to tell you this, Ryan, but the Lord has been whispering to me all week: *Ryan's project needs to die.*"

The death theme could not have been any clearer. At this point, three people (one of them me!) had the same vision: a dead project. But I *still* wasn't ready to raise the white flag—I was clutching this idea with all the white-knuckled hope I had. So I fought back.

"You tell me what that means! Because I still have a quarter-of-a-million-dollar loan out on this project that's incurring interest every single day, Kelsey. So I need to know what you mean when you say it needs to die!"

"I think it needs to die in our hearts, Ryan. It's too important to us. We've made an idol out of this project and our desire for its potential success. It's too big, taking up too much of us. We need to let it go."

"Okay, okay, it can die in my heart!" I yelled back, internally vowing to somehow make this documentary less important to me and my identity if God would still allow it to happen, still get us on a platform for the world to see. But as Kelsey and I continued to talk, I started to realize that wasn't going to be possible.

"I really think we need to pull it," she said. "Maybe it's for a season. Maybe it's forever. I don't know. But the only obedience I can see going forward is to stop."

I hung up the phone angry, frustrated, and undeniably scared about the conviction in my heart.

The changes in my thinking that followed did not happen instantly, and I will not say they happened easily either. But in the moments that followed this conversation, I started to reluctantly embrace what I knew was true: The project was done.

Kelsey and I called our agents back and said, "We've decided we are no longer going to pursue this." They were undeniably confused. Here we were, these little documentary makers who had a chance to make it big, telling them, "We're going to push pause on this." It was humiliating, but it was the right thing to do.

After that, I had to have the same conversations with a whole lot of other people, and honestly, this was even harder. There were so many stakeholders and investors—people who had given a lot of money—not to mention those who knew the project was well underway and cared about its success. And I had to communicate to all of them that we were canceling it.

Every single one of them was confused. I could envision them rolling their eyes at me, saying, "*You heard from God and now you're no longer moving forward with this million-dollar project?*"

"*Listen, I get it,*" I'd reply. If I hadn't heard so clearly and undeniably from the Lord, I probably would have had the same reaction. But it *was* clear.

Then there was the money. To make the documentary, I'd taken out a $250,000 loan—the one accruing interest—from a foundation. But within days of us telling our agents to stop moving forward, a check for the exact amount I owed that foundation showed up in the mail. Like, what?! Only God could do that. I know it was his way of telling me, "Look, I paid this debt for you. Now you have absolutely no excuse to keep holding on to this, even in your heart. It's really done, Ryan."

But the toughest conversation I needed to have was still ahead of me.

At the same time that I was pursuing the documentary, I had started an online mental health support ministry. Even though one dream had died, I believed that the ministry should keep going. And I needed more funding to make that happen.

So I went back to one of the biggest donors, a man who was both generous and kind, who loved our family, and who I thought would be willing to support this work because he believed in it—and in me. He was someone important to me, but he had clearly communicated his hesitancy about us ending the documentary project. I knew he was not fully on board with our decision and that he didn't understand the deep conviction in our hearts that God was putting a stop to it. But I still believed he trusted me.

When I got him on the phone one afternoon, I boldly asked him for more funding. He stopped me abruptly. "Ryan, I've given you a million dollars of our money, and you've done nothing with it. You're feeding dog food to dogs who don't even like the taste of the food. I'm not giving you another dime." It was honest, direct, and incredibly hard to hear.

I put the phone on mute and started crying. This was a man I would have done anything to impress. He had invested so much in me. To hear his disappointment devastated me. It was many of my worst fears coming true: *You lost our money. You screwed everything up. You're a failure.*

This is where things really started to crumble. I thought for sure the ministry was going to be another item on my failure list, and I started spiraling. The public nature of much of this only added to my shame.

I didn't know what I was doing with my life. I kept failing. I told Annie at one point, "I think I might be depressed," and my body carried on like I truly was: no energy, no joy, and a constant stream of negative thoughts about myself to go with it.

When Connor, my mentor, told me to go burrow under a mountain, it scared me. Because it wasn't just that he was offering me some advice I should consider. It truly felt like he was prophesying over me. "You *need* to burrow under a mountain." As in: This was not optional. In my heart, I heard his words, but really, I was thinking, *You don't understand, Connor. This show is popping off right now. We are on our way! What I need right now is the opposite of burrowing, I need to grow!*

But the Lord, in his kindness, took away the renown, the project, and every opportunity with it. It really was time to burrow under the mountain. A few months later, still feeling lost and like a shell of my former self, I started going out on long hikes to spend time with the Lord, just me and Jesus. I had no plan for the next step in my life, no idea what it would look like to start over. I simply had the gift of obscurity and the blessing of enough time to walk and talk with the Lord.

Slowly, I started healing.

After I shared with him some of what God was teaching me during those hikes, my buddy said, "You know, I wonder, while you're having these talks with Jesus, if you've ever thought of recording some of them and maybe sharing them on social media or something? Because this is some rich stuff. I think it could bless others."

I thought if I was going to have an audience, it was going to be through my work at the ranch as the mentor who "knew it all." Instead, my friend's suggestion opened a door I had never even thought of. In that desperate, searching, waiting season, the Lord lovingly pushed me to the beauty of the whole and simple gospel: I am more broken and sinful than I ever dared imagine, and more loved and cherished than I ever dared believe.[5] As a creator and a communicator at heart, I may not have had a big project to focus on, but man, I still had a desire to make something with purpose.

The whole and simple gospel meant everything to me. Jesus meant everything to me. And I wanted to share that with others. So I thought about what my friend said and started making short videos—in real time, on these hikes in the wilderness with God, unfiltered and unscripted—about all the things the Lord was teaching me.

The videos started gaining traction. The gospel was going viral! Within a year, I had almost a million followers watching these simple videos, filmed from hiking trails, the front seat of my car, and while walking out of a coffee shop. It was the least edited version of myself I had ever been—but the most desperate for Jesus I'd ever been too.

Like many of us, I have always wanted to matter, to be known. But I wanted to be known for doing big things, not losing big dreams. Yet it was in the loss that I truly found the presence of God. He was what I had been chasing all along. Before this, I had been looking for fool's gold, but those "riches" that I desperately wanted were chopped from my life. God allowed me to be embarrassed and ashamed so I could understand my complete inability to make anything of myself apart from his grace. The Lord made me wait on him in order to teach me a little more of what I needed to know. And he's certainly not done with me either.

THE LONGER THE WAIT

The reason why the Greeks wanted tamed horses from the wild over any other type of horse is not merely because they were tougher than the others. They made the best warhorses because of the unwinding and reframing that happened in their struggle. All that time spent in the round pen—kicking and bucking, fighting for autonomy and control, wishing to go back to the independence of the wild—brought them slowly, painfully, and beautifully to the place where they recognized their need for utter dependence on their master.

The Greek soldiers knew it took longer to tame a horse to be ready for war, but it was worth it. The wilder the animal, the longer the wait. But if that soldier could capture that horse's heart, he was rewarded with a horse that would do anything, go anywhere, and love that master through any battle they might face. That would be the joy of the soldier, to have an unbreakable bond forged by years of training. Although the horse didn't know it in the round pen, this submission and dependence would yield far greater joy than chasing the freedom it thought it wanted for all that time.

DON'T TAKE YOUR PRESENCE

In Psalm 51, David wrote a prayer of repentance and lament. He had been caught in an adulterous relationship, had the husband of his mistress murdered, and generally been so drunk on power that he used it for abusive and destructive purposes. When the prophet Nathan confronted him and called him out on his awful choices, he didn't defend himself or stew in anger. He turned back to his first love and his most natural mode of communication with God: songs of prayer.

> Have mercy on me, O God,
>   according to your unfailing love;
> according to your great compassion
>   blot out my transgressions.
> Wash away all my iniquity
>   and cleanse me from my sin.
>
> For I know my transgressions,
>   and my sin is always before me.
> Against you, you only, have I sinned
>   and done what is evil in your sight;
> so you are right in your verdict
>   and justified when you judge. . . .

Create in me a pure heart, O God,
    and renew a steadfast spirit within me.
Do not cast me from your presence
    or take your Holy Spirit from me.
Restore to me the joy of your salvation
    and grant me a willing spirit, to sustain me.[6]

David was the king. He had absolutely everything: wealth, power, family, respect. But he didn't beg to keep any of these things. He's saying in this prayer, "If I can ask you to leave me with one thing, God, it's not going to be my throne, my crown, or my title. It's just your presence. Please don't leave me, God."

David understood what seasons in the wilderness show us: Yes, we might have to surrender the thing we want most. But take that thing away and only then do we understand that what we *really* want and need most is the presence of Jesus. It's his meek heart that we are after. A willingness to surrender and wait is vital to experiencing more of him.

MEEK MOMENT

There are two mindsets in life that keep us stuck. The first is looking back—like Lot's wife, frozen in nostalgia or regret. The second is looking too far ahead—caught in the fog of the what-ifs. Both steal us from the present moment, where the Kingdom of God actually lives. Because the Kingdom resides in the what-is: whatever is true, whatever is noble, whatever is lovely, whatever is excellent and praiseworthy. And when we think on these things, his peace that surpasses understanding guards our hearts and minds in Christ Jesus.[7]

My prayer for you today is this: that you would not fear the pruning of the Lord or despise the wilderness. That you would trust him day by day for your manna and quail. And when those wilderness seasons come—and they will—you would remember that they are for your formation, not your failure.

Early in his call from the Lord, Moses said, "If your presence doesn't go with me, I don't want to go."[8] He couldn't have known that decades later, the presence of the Lord would truly be all he had. Moses never made it to the land flowing with milk and honey. After everything—dismissals from Pharaoh, the miracle on the Red Sea, daily provision, forty years of leading millions of people—Moses' sins still had consequences.

Deuteronomy 32 explains, "Both of you [Moses and his brother, Aaron] broke faith with me among the Israelites at the Waters of Meribath-kadesh in the Wilderness of Zin by failing to treat me as holy in their presence. Although from a distance you will view the land that I am giving the Israelites, you will not go there."[9]

Moses never got "the thing," that elusive prize or goal—whatever it may be—that we think we need to feel content. But he *always* had God's presence. He wasn't perfect, but Scripture goes on to tell us what a truly mighty man of God he was, that "no prophet has risen in Israel like Moses, whom the Lord knew face to face, who did all those signs and wonders the Lord sent him to do in Egypt. . . . No one has ever shown the mighty power or performed the awesome deeds that Moses did in the sight of all Israel."[10]

Were those forty years of waiting and wondering and wandering in the desert a waste? Not if God is who he says he is. Remember, God was the one who led the Israelites into the wilderness. In order for God to get the Israelites out of Egypt, he had to get Egypt out of the Israelites, and that was not going to be a quick fix. Changing long-held habits, reforming thought patterns, and teaching new ways of seeing and living, along with being in a brand-new place with new rules and new roles, could not happen overnight. Not for the Israelites, and certainly not for us. God is always doing something new in us as we wait, but the gift is that he *is* still with us.

The gift for Moses was never the Promised Land. It was God.

THE KID WITH THE BACKPACK

I told my friend Reid, the one who had the vision of me as a wacky inflatable man, about some of the things I was learning on my hikes. Reid, always the faithful friend, told me that he had actually seen a vision of me again while he was praying for me. In this one, I started as the big, strong superhero, but instead of deflating into the wacky inflatable guy, I turned into my high school self. I was just a kid with a backpack and a big smile on my face. Reid said, "I saw you with this backpack slung over your shoulders, and you turned back to me with an almost giddy grin on your face. Then without hesitation, you turned your back on me and walked straight into the desert by yourself. You were excited, like that was the only place you wanted to be." It was the affirmation I needed to remind myself of what I knew to be true: There is not one season of our lives that God is going to waste.

As I look back on that deeply challenging season of life when I was letting go of some of my dreams and burrowing under the mountain, it's clear that God had plenty to teach me about my own heart when he's not truly at the center. It would be arrogant of me to think that because of the way God has used me since then, I'm good to go—refined during the wilderness of waiting and now off and running into a lifetime of influence. Yes, I do have more influence today than I used to. People do know my name. And God could take it all away again in a second if he wanted to, and that would be okay. Because all I really want is him.

We can't strategize our way through waiting, and we can't attempt to bypass the wilderness God leads us to. In fact, any attempted shortcuts will probably prolong our journey. Why? Because it's really not about the destination. It's about what God is doing in us on the way there. His will is going to be accomplished, and he doesn't *need* us to do anything for him. The Bible is one long story of God's people really messing up what they were supposed to do for God and him constantly course-correcting everyone. We jump off the track; God lifts us up and puts us back on.

But he is, graciously and almost unfathomably, pleased to use us for his purposes if we will cultivate the meekness to live on mission for him. And meekness is forged in the waiting, in the seasons of our lives when our need for the Lord can't be filled with anything else, when we can't distract ourselves with anything the world has to offer. We get a taste of true meekness in those elusive moments in life where nothing but Jesus will suffice.

CHAPTER 8

A NEW OPERATING SYSTEM

Behold, I am doing a new thing; now it springs forth, do you not perceive it?

I will make a way in the wilderness and rivers in the desert.

ISAIAH 43:19, ESV

I can still recall the feeling of the thin foam of the pink yoga mat underneath my nose and forehead. This mat was the only barrier between the weight of my full body and my living room's floor as I lay face-first on the ground, arms heavy to my side, sick with anxiety. Lying there on the floor had become a regular part of the morning for me, somehow a physical representation of the desperation and tension that my mind could not seem to kick. The documentary I had put everything into—time, money, and the resources of so many people—was a dead project. And my sense of purpose, along with my ego, seemed to die right along with it.

It took me some time to understand what God was doing, to see the self-centric cycle he was pulling me out of. I tried many different things to get my head on straight. I tried acupuncture—which was terrible and painful because I was so tense from anxiety that none of my muscles would relax enough for that treatment to be anything but torture. I tried giving myself miniature pep talks, offering condolences to my brain like, *You're still a good person!* and, *You can try again next time!* While both of those thoughts were not entirely untrue, they were entirely inadequate. As human beings, we are not capable of giving ourselves a new heart; only God can do that. The trite things we tell ourselves in an effort to feel better always come up short.

It was in that season of so much time on that pink yoga mat, while I was asking God over and over again, *What are you doing in me?* that God started whispering the word meekness to me.

At first, I wondered if the Lord was using the work meek as a rebuke. Was my personality too abrasive? Was God disciplining me because I was too hardened and prideful? Was the antidote simply to shut up and learn to be quieter, less ambitious, "more meek"—at least as I understood the word at the time? But when the whispers wouldn't let up, I followed them. Soon enough, I was like an eager puppy on the hunt for a bone, relentlessly looking everywhere for what it meant to be truly meek. I found every use of the word in Scripture that I could, cross-referenced the terms in their original languages, and studied the context of those uses. I couldn't get enough of the chase. It was healing me. Before losing a big dream, I didn't realize how broken and unhealthy parts of my life were.

Ultimately it was finding out the deeper meaning of the Greek word *praus* that turned the Lord's whispers into a shout. There I was, regularly reduced to tears of brokenness on a yoga mat, hearing the Lord say, *Meekness*, over and over. I was perhaps the only person in the world with the unique context of having recently lost a million-dollar project centered on taming wild mustangs. And right there, as I studied meekness, I saw it. The word *praus*, often translated as *meek* in Scripture,[1] has a revealing word picture attached to it: In other Greek writings, it is sometimes used to describe tamed warhorses.[2]

My chase to understand meekness went from hungry to ravenous.

I decided I needed to find the meekest people on the planet and talk to them about their lives. I have a friend who worked for many years in a high-level government agency—someone who has been at every professional mountaintop you could probably imagine and is a Spirit-filled man of great faith. To me, he embodies a wild mustang who has been tamed for the Lord's purposes. When I told him about what had transpired in the months before—all the losses and embarrassment leading to my desperation to hear from God—he saw the fire the Lord had put in me to understand meekness. And he knew I wasn't going to learn about it simply by reading more books and articles. He knew that even though I have more life to live and more wilderness to walk through, I needed to hear from people whose stories and experiences I would never have.

So my friend put me in touch with one of his colleagues, Aaron. Aaron is one of those people that could scare you just by being in the same room as you. He's strong, almost imposing, and his confidence is hard won. Aaron has been in some of the toughest places in the world, worked in the most dangerous circumstances, and yet, there's not one part of him that is trying to impress anyone with his stories. He simply shares what happened, never juicing the details for a reaction from listeners. And while he might be intimidating, he's the kind of guy who makes you sit up and lean in a little closer as you listen to him.

Aaron patiently let me tell him all about my new pursuit of meekness. I told him how I couldn't shake the idea that we had it all wrong—that meekness isn't an insulting characteristic or the demeanor of someone who lacks courage but rather is strength under control. I couldn't shut up, my enthusiasm running away with my words. "We've got to learn to really surrender our lives!" I told him, anxious for the affirmation of his response, hoping maybe my zeal would impress him.

Aaron listened to me, likely entertained by the naive twenty-eight-year-old in front of him. But he was not impressed. He finally stopped me and said, "Ryan, you keep using the word surrender when you talk about meekness, but I think there is a better word than surrender." Then he proceeded to tell me about a moment that revealed a whole new category to meekness.

Aaron had spent time in Afghanistan, and his tenure there spanned a season when the US Army was training Afghan resistance fighters to band against the Soviet army in the wake of the Soviet invasion of 1979.

"We were training these resistance fighters to fight the Soviet army, so it's my job to show them how to be a warrior, right? Well, these guys were so gnarly, so warrior-like in their attitude of total abandon already, every time they would hear a Soviet helicopter coming, in unison they would run outside, point their rifles toward the sky, and start shooting haphazardly at the helicopter, as if that would do anything. Their fervor couldn't be held back. The helicopter would rain down fire in return, but these men didn't care. I would be screaming, 'Take cover! Take cover!' But they wouldn't ever take cover, and it drove me crazy. They believed deeply that they had already lost their lives to their cause. So if their physical bodies were taken too—well, they anticipated that.

"As I was yelling at these men to get back to safety, to rein in the fervor that sent them like kamikazes out into the desert with absolutely no shot of coming back victorious, the Holy Spirit tapped me on the shoulder and said, 'Aaron, these men are lost and misguided. *But they are meeker than you, because they've lost their lives while you are still holding on to yours.* You haven't given it all to me yet.' That's when the Lord made meekness come alive to me. It's more than surrender. *It's about who owns you.* And really, for followers of Christ, it's losing ownership of our lives completely."

Listening to Aaron recount this story for me, I realized he was right. I could get on board with surrender, but in my mind, surrender meant "Use my life *as it is* already, God. If you could just keep all the dreams and plans I have for my life the same, but use them to glorify your name, I surrender those dreams and plans to you." If I was going to truly understand what Jesus had for me in my pursuit of a lost and misunderstood virtue, I had to go deeper and be far more willing to put my entire life, along with every desire and everything God had given me, on the altar. I had to learn to trade out all my old ways of thinking for brand-new ones. I needed an entirely new operating system.

MEEK MOMENT

If you've ever spent much time in the metaphorical round pen with the Lord, you know that losing ownership can feel like a part of you is dying. It's uncomfortable, because everything you've known begins to change. The way you've made decisions, the way you've called the shots, it's all in the past now.

The round pen is uncomfortable. And much like I was on my journey, maybe you are still working out this newfound meekness with the Lord. You have lost your life, and that's the point. The transfer of ownership has changed into the rightful, capable, loving hands of your Father, and you are becoming more yielded to his will for you by the day.

OUR DEFAULT MODE

There are two operating systems we all have: fear and love. When we start from a place of fear, everything we do is motivated by self-preservation and protection. Our eyes are on ourselves, and we focus on doing what it takes to get ahead and stay ahead at all costs. But when we start operating from a place of love, our choices and actions are motivated by the needs of others and gratitude.

The problem is that the default mode of the human heart can be summed up in one word: self. If Satan can get us to focus on ourselves, our lives, our problems, our concerns, our worries, if he can distract us with enough self-focus, he's won. His schemes are far more slippery and sinister than anything as obvious as witchcraft or "Satan worship." Those things are present in the world, but the majority of people never even need to encounter either to be totally deceived. Satan loves when our life motto is as unobjectionable as "Do what thou wilt."[3] This motto, in its various forms, tones, and wordings, has become the anthem of our world. "Listen to your heart! God just wants you to be happy!" But these sentiments, and the results of living them out, are dangerous distractions from pursuing Christ.

In Philippians 2, Paul is writing a letter to the church in Philippi—a letter that could be considered one of Christianity's "greatest hits" for its quotable nature and one-line zingers. But it's so important, vital even, to the impact of this letter to know that Paul wrote it from prison.

Literally behind heavy metal bars, starving, filthy, beaten, and mocked. First-century prisons were riddled with diseases and grime, places of constant death and torture. The kind of circumstances we can hardly imagine even looking at were the backdrop of Paul's letter, a piece that opens with the words "I *thank* my God every time I remember you. In all my prayers for all of you, *I always pray with joy*."[4] I complain when it's too hot outside. It's hard to imagine the kind of Holy Spirit intervention it would take for most of us to be thankful in a dirty and dangerous jail cell.

As Paul encourages followers of Jesus in this small church to live their lives "worthy of the gospel of Christ," he leads them away from the idea that our culture today wants to hammer into everyone.[5] Every self-help book in the world will tell you a dozen ways to flourish by focusing on your own self-preservation. But Paul tells us to "do *nothing* out of selfish ambition or vain conceit. Rather, in humility value others above yourselves."[6]

The world says, "Do what thou wilt." The Bible says, "Do *nothing* for yourself, but do what God wilt." It's the most important reframing of our lives.

FALL FROM HEAVEN

Consistent self-focus has led us into mental, emotional, and spiritual disarray. It's the very thing that led to the fall in Genesis 3—when sin entered the world for the first time through the choices of two people who wanted more than

God had provided already—and its damage continues, hidden in plain sight, disguised as self-help or positive phraseology. This mindset has spread its poison in every industry; planted misleading seeds about purpose, identity, and success in the minds of our youth; skewed our understanding of identity, sexuality, and relationships.

Satan wants us to mimic his core identity of self-worship and unending pride. In Luke 10, seventy-two of Jesus' disciples were returning from missionary work all over the region, not complaining of their hardships but rejoicing in the success of their work. They said, "Lord, even the demons submit to us in your name."[7] Jesus' response? It wasn't a high five or a "See, I told you guys it would work!" I imagine Jesus with a deadpan face, looking back at his disciples who had a skip in their step and pride in their retellings and saying, "I saw Satan fall like lightning from heaven."[8]

What? Here the disciples must have been expecting a proud teacher who would be thrilled at the work his students had produced. Instead, we don't see a commendation or a trophy but a warning. It's as if Jesus could sense the way pride was sneaking into their hearts, the small and subtle ways they were feeling impressed with themselves for their influence and power. He continued, "Do not rejoice that the spirits submit to you, but rejoice that your names are written in heaven."[9]

The reason Satan fell like lightning was because he could never move past the question "When is it going to be about me?" Satan cloaks his pursuit of separating people from

God by getting them to live out "the gospel of self" because he knows it's the most destructive. Individualism is his master plan, disguised everywhere you look: social media, the entertainment world, self-help programs, and even well-meaning Christian advice. It's so sneaky we hardly recognize it anymore. And yet the mindset every one of us can be tempted toward—the *But look how important I am!* desires of our hearts—is what banished Satan from the presence of a holy God.

WHO OWNS YOU?

I don't own my life. It's not mine and never has been. I lose my life, putting myself and every dream I have for my future on the altar, and then the Lord gives it back to me tenfold through himself.[10] That's the upside-down nature of following a carpenter and Shepherd who is also a King—his way doesn't make logical sense, until you realize by faith that it's the *only* thing that makes sense.

What Aaron saw in those Afghan resistance fighters was a true willingness to lose their lives. Their ultimate sacrifice was misguided in every way—from the god they believed in to their reckless actions. Still, Aaron couldn't help but wonder, *What if followers of Jesus, who not only had the truth of Jesus' gospel but also the model of laying down one's life in sacrificial love rather than self-glory seeking retribution, had this same willingness to turn over everything in their lives for a grander purpose?*

A mustang in the wild lives out of a sense of fear and self-preservation. A human being does too. Until they meet Jesus.

Once a mustang is tamed, gentled, and taught to trust the authority who has shown him patient, enduring love, the mustang is ready to be led in willing obedience into a greater purpose than self-preservation.

What if, just as a tamed mustang must learn to live with an entirely new operating system, Christians understood that the call of Christ demands a new operating system too? One grounded in the purest form of love we could ever know, a love that does not seek to preserve our own lives but rather to put our lives on the altar so that God can do what he wills with them? Imagine it: a world full of Christ followers who truly believe that "to live is Christ and to die is gain."[11] Everything would change.

Revelation says, "They [believers] conquered him [Satan] by the blood of the Lamb and by the word of their testimony; for they did not love their lives to the point of death."[12] As believers, we will overcome when we lay down our lives for Christ's cause. Seventeenth-century theologian Matthew Henry comments on this passage: "Their love to their own lives was overcome by *stronger affections* of another nature; and this their courage and zeal helped to confound their enemies, to convince many of the spectators, to confirm the souls of the faithful, and so contributed greatly to this victory."[13] Henry is saying that having a stronger desire for eternal life than we do for this life on earth *is the new operating system*. And it's one of the fruits of pursuing meekness.

Aaron was on track to lead a large division of the US Army, with responsibilities and respect that most people can only dream of in a vocation. He had earned the right to be considered for one of the most influential and powerful roles in the US government. But because his new role would be asking him to make decisions that conflicted too profoundly with his faith in Jesus, Aaron turned down the opportunity. He could do this with peace and freedom because he had already lost ownership. His life really wasn't his own. Losing ownership is still the chase I am on every day. I've tasted moments of the freedom of true meekness, of what it's like to live with a new operating system, to make decisions that are more focused on God's glory than anything else. But I have to fight my own sin every single day. I'm tempted toward distraction, to idolize the wrong things, to misplace my priorities. It's been years since I was face down on the yoga mat. But even today, as I write this book, I can tend to spin myself into the ground going after the wrong things.

I recently spent some time with former pro football player James, a man who reached the pinnacle of his sports career but almost took his own life when he discovered after climbing to the top of the mountain that there was nothing up there. But God intervened, and James was rescued by the grace of Jesus. Today, he runs an influential ministry for men and powerfully speaks into others' lives.

James invited me to an early morning prayer time, where a bunch of men gathered together to listen to God and one another. As James was praying for me, he stopped and said,

"Ryan, I just got a vision: It's you standing alone on a football field, surrounded by the expanse of the stadium and the roar of the crowd. But you have an IV in your arm, and it's hooked up to the scoreboard."

The image stopped me in my tracks. Through the discernment of the Holy Spirit, James had nailed it; he'd nailed me. Having my vocation and identity connected to followers, numbers, and the opinion of others, and allowing my contentment and confidence to rise and fall along with them, is exactly what I struggle with. It's the source of one of the greatest anxieties of my life. I'm afraid to fail, so I connect my worth to metrics, to whether I'm successful in reaching a whole lot of people.

James looked at me and said, "It's like that scoreboard is your operating system, as though life and death for you depend on those numbers. Ryan, I think you need a completely different operating system."

James didn't know that I was working on this exact chapter when he challenged me with that image. God continues to blow me away with the ever-present realization that even though I am writing this book, I'm not all the way to meekness yet and I probably won't be in this lifetime. And the Lord is going to ask me to keep living this message, no matter how many moments I might arrogantly think, *I got it. I've arrived at meekness.*

The Christian life and the pursuit of Jesus means losing ownership of everything you want, picking up your cross, and running toward whatever Jesus puts in front of you.

Pursuing influence, though, means doing whatever it takes to gain more followers, because you believe *that* is what you want. And the scary truth is I still care about what the world thinks of me too much. But Jesus wanted nothing from the world. Jesus was *truly* meek; he had fully lost ownership of his life. There is a small part of me that wants to believe, like Adam and Eve, that I can have a little bit of the glory that belongs to God. I'm still getting my old operating system of "self" sanctified out of me.

MEEK MOMENT

The best thing you can do when you come to the end of yourself is to fall back into God's loving arms. You are like a caterpillar becoming a butterfly. You are like John, the Son of Thunder, becoming the disciple Jesus loved. And this transformation is a beautiful thing. Praise the Lord for the change he's creating in you:

> *Jesus, thank you for my yielded life. Would you honor my decision to lay it all down for you? Would you increase the dividend of your presence day by day as I seek to become meek and lowly? Allow me to see that meekness is how I was truly designed to live. And though it feels awkward in the transition right now, fill me with hope for the future—a vision for the life outside the round pen, fully alive and fully yours.*
>
> *Amen.*

BECOMING SOMEONE NEW

In the past few months, my wife, Annie, and I have had to work through a season of more bickering and arguing than is normal for us. We have four young kids, so exhaustion and stress are real contributors to that, but we both know it is not *just* the reality of life with young, busy, loud kids.

It's also that God is doing a new thing in Annie. He's changing out an old operating system of fear for one that is far more freeing for her.

With the help of a trusted counselor, Annie and I began to process what is going on in her and how it is changing us as a couple. Here is what it comes down to: Annie is finding her voice, and I have to learn to hear it.

Annie's story is hers to tell, but in a lot of ways, she grew up not believing that she had the right to be heard, even in her own home. And then she married me—someone who has always wanted to be heard—and with trust and love for each other, we almost unconsciously assumed these roles in our marriage, because they seemed to match our natural dispositions.

As life has gotten fuller and busier, with the demands on our schedules pulling us in different directions, God has begun to help Annie understand that she *does* have a voice and permission to use it. She needs to use it. Because God loves Annie, and because Annie loves me, she *gets* to speak into my life, into our marriage, and into the direction our work and family go. She didn't believe this confidently about herself a few years ago, but as the counselor told us, "Annie has been in a chrysalis, and while the growth that happens there is vital to the life after, it can be painful to come out of that chrysalis and take in the new person that you are." There have been moments of pain, and certainly moments of tension, as we figure out how God is making *both* of us more gracious communicators: her with more courage, me with more humility.

But what I have seen in my bride is this: She has changed. Out of generous love for his daughter, God did something beautiful in her confidence, giving her the voice I need in my life, that our family needs forever. As Annie sees and understands more and more this new operating system of love from the Lord, everyone around her is better for her influence and for the voice she didn't know she was allowed to use. Meekness is about the heart of Christ, which means the changes God does in someone aren't always going to be about taming the wild. He empowers the scared too.

Jesus came to reveal the heart of his Father, not to show how eloquent his teachings were or how charismatic he was. My motives, on the other hand, will always be tainted and impure, and it's a grace that the Lord has given me a platform where I am constantly confronted with how not-meek I really am, with how much I desire to be "enough."

Yet I believe the pursuit of meekness is changing me, making me more into the man God has called me to be. And I'm determined to listen, to lose ownership, to invite the Lord to give me a new operating system every single day until I'm home with him.

CHAPTER 9

UNOFFENDABLE

The fear of man lays a snare, but whoever trusts in the LORD *is safe.*

PROVERBS 29:25, ESV

When was the last time you felt offended? Was it an offhand comment a coworker made while trying to be funny or a political advertisement espousing a view different from your own? How about a comment left on your social media post or something a perfect stranger wrote on their own page about their epic new wellness routine? If we are honest, we could all probably name something that offends or bothers us. And most of the time, it's the little "somethings" that add up and chip away at our good attitudes.

I think it's clear: We are easily offended people, and we easily offend others.

There's something behind offendability that is deeper than having thin skin or being extra irritable some days.

We desire to be seen, loved, and respected, and when we don't feel like we are, our attitudes can become resentful or annoyed at what we perceive to be an insult.

No one is exempt from this. The human condition of sin that we are all born with means our thoughts are preoccupied with, mostly, *ourselves* and how everything in life affects *us*. We obsess over self-image and how highly (or not) other people think of us. We interpret and weigh events by how they directly or indirectly influence our circumstances. It's a problem we all live with.

But our hearts don't have to stay this way, not if meekness is the pursuit of our lives. Because when we desire to live a meek life, we aren't preoccupied with the need to be loved. Meek people focus on *becoming love*. In fact, like the mustang won over by the gentleness of his tamer, meek people are so filled with God's love that they are not concerned with what others think of them; their primary concern is to embody and live out love to others.

BECOMING LOVE—CAROLE'S STORY

One of the most profound examples I have ever seen of a meek, gospel-humble person—someone who has fully replaced the need to defend themselves with a Holy Spirit–inspired desire to love others—is my friend Carole Ward.

Carole is a third-generation missionary who grew up in the Philippines in a militant Muslim area, where her parents served with Wycliffe Bible Translators. Her childhood was spent playing games and making memories in the jungle with the children of ISIS members. Carole's early experiences shaped the longing of her heart to reach the most unreached people groups in the world with the Word of God.

In 2002, the Lord opened the door for Carole to serve in southern Uganda. At this time, the Lord's Resistance Army was terrorizing the region of northern Uganda, pillaging villages and abducting children by the tens of thousands, forcing them to become child soldiers and sex slaves. Their rule was nothing short of demonic, and most people were running *from* it. But as this war in the north claimed thousands of lives, and as missions organizations, government agencies, and Westerners were leaving the war zone, Carole knew God was calling her to draw closer *to* it. She moved into the area to pray and to live.[1] Her cry was "Lord, would you give me a bucket of water and a towel so I can walk through the land and wash the feet of men and women who have walked in suffering that I'll never understand?"[2]

How does someone find that kind of courage? Before getting to know Carole, I might have said that she could do these mighty things for Jesus because her faith was so grand, so much bigger than her fear. But it's not *just* that. Carole's fear has been completely consumed by love, and her story leaves me speechless even now.

"I saw in my father a tremendous amount of faith, a tremendous amount of love, and a tremendous amount of boldness—he had no fear," Carole said. "You can't have boldness if you have fear. I realized his boldness and spiritual authority came from his *love* for the people. He was willing to lay down his life for them, like John 15 says. I had this modeled in front of me every day.

"I really believe that the great commandment—which is to love the Lord your God with all of your heart, soul, strength, and mind, and then your neighbor as yourself—leads us to the great commission, where it is the driving force for each one of our missions. If we don't have that driving force . . . fear will paralyze us."

Carole went on to tell me, "As I was driving north [into Uganda], I was fighting with so much fear, driving through a war zone where I was surrounded by bombed vehicles and where guerrillas would often jump out and stop your car, pull you out, and kill you right there; of course I was afraid. And I heard the Lord say, *I can't use you with fear.* So I thought, *Okay, Lord, then I need more faith. Would you give me more faith?* But what I heard from God changed that request: *You have faith, Carole. You are obeying me by going into this very dangerous place. What you need is more love.*

"And I prayed, *Lord, would you baptize me in love? Enough love to trust you with my life, and enough love to go serve and lay my life down for the people I am going to see, to count them more important than my own self-preservation.* And he did. Right there, he baptized me in love, and you know what? I haven't felt fear since."[3]

Can you imagine that kind of freedom? Most of us don't have a day that goes by where we don't experience fear, even in small ways. I know I certainly don't! I wrestle with some kind of fear multiple times a day: fear of others' opinions of me, fear of failure, fear of any number of circumstances or possibilities. And yet, unlike many of us, Carole has learned, by God's grace, that the true antidote to fear is not becoming more popular by pleasing the masses, or mustering up more bravery, or padding our bank accounts for a larger financial safety net, or surrounding ourselves with people who regularly do daring things, like jumping out of airplanes or scuba diving in undersea caves. The antidote is, quite simply, love.

MEEK MOMENT

Few of us will experience stories like Carole's in our lifetimes, and that's okay! Most of us have a life that looks a bit more like showing up to a corporate job or taking care of kids all day. But more of us *could* have a life that testifies to Jesus, even in days far more ordinary than Carole's drive into a war zone.

Regardless of where we live, the love of Jesus is irresistible and true. There are so many people who walk through life restless and offendable. The world can't help but notice people who live selflessly, who have become love. Jesus went on trial for us. He took the beating we deserved. And that means the verdict about our "goodness" is in: If we are found in Christ, we are alright. More than alright, because we have *his* righteousness. In order to live this out, as Timothy

Keller writes, "We have to re-live the gospel every time we pray."[4] Take a moment to reflect on Jesus' sacrifice for us. Then pray that he would baptize you in love today.

WHEN PEOPLE ARE TOO PRIDEFUL

When it comes to fear and offendability, the question we all have to ask ourselves is this: *Who or what do I spend the most time thinking about?* For most of us, the honest answer would be our own finger pointed right back at ourselves. We are a human race obsessed with self-image and with the conclusions the people around us draw about who we are. As believers, most of us are sure God loves us, but if we are honest, that knowledge is rarely enough. We want recognition, love, respect, and admiration from other people. We love God but need people. And that's the problem: What or who we need will control us. It will underlie our motivations, direct our choices, and cloud the boundary lines of our lives. We often chase others' praise because we think that will finally satisfy the deep longings in our hearts. But that's where we go wrong: The more we chase the approval of others, the more angst we uncover in ourselves.

In his classic book on the fear of man, author Edward Welch defines the phrase like this: "The fear of man can be summarized this way: *We replace God with people.*"[5] He goes on to say, "Fear of man is part of our human fabric. How nice it would be to actually feel comfortable in our own skin rather than needing to *be* somebody or searching for that drop of love or sliver of approval from someone."[6]

This is not a new problem. Since sin entered the world, "we see God less clearly and are less attentive to him, but we are acutely, if not painfully, aware of other people's [opinions]."[7] The Bible is full of examples of people who struggled with this, and full of warnings about the cost.

HARD LESSONS

In 1 Samuel 15:1-24, we read that what truly cost Saul his position as king over Israel was a greater fear of what the people would think of him than submission to what God told him to do. In this passage, Saul was told through the prophet Samuel, "Go and strike Amalek and devote to destruction all that they have. Do not spare them."[8] It was a direct command from the Lord, his clear instructions on what to do to this enemy because of the opposition they displayed to Israel when they came out of Egypt. In order to seek justice, Saul did lead Israel into battle against the Amalekites, and he defeated them. But then, "Saul and the people spared Agag and the best of the sheep and of the oxen and of the fattened calves and the lambs, and all that was good, and would not utterly destroy them."[9]

Saul obeyed *almost* all the way. But *almost* still misses the mark completely. In fact, it's in those *almost* moments that the most egregious sins against a holy God can be committed.

When Samuel confronted Saul for failing to do all that the Lord commanded him to do, Saul immediately took offense. "Whoa, relax, Samuel! I did what God told me to do!"[10] And yet Samuel, like the parent who has caught their child with a candy bar in his back pocket while insisting he didn't steal it, was having none of it. "Why do I hear all these animals around, then? Where did you get them from, Saul?" And so, Saul started to concede. "Well, some of the people I brought with me may or may not have spared some of the good stuff. You know, like only the best sheep and oxen. But! We are going to sacrifice them to the Lord our God! So really, it's all good, right, Samuel?"[11]

No. It's not all good. "Then Samuel said to Saul, 'Stop! I will tell you what the LORD said to me this night.'"[12]

Picture Samuel with his hand in Saul's face, more or less telling him he can shut up now. Can you imagine the boldness of Samuel in this moment? He was an old man, but he commanded the respect of the people, and he was the one person who could still tell Saul what to do. And he essentially told Saul to sit down like a child—I imagine the throne felt more like a time-out chair at this moment—stop talking, and listen. Saul needed to understand what he'd really done.

> Has the LORD as great delight in burnt offerings and
>   sacrifices,
>   as in obeying the voice of the LORD?
> Behold, to obey is better than sacrifice,
>   and to listen than the fat of rams.
> For rebellion is as the sin of divination,
>   and presumption is as iniquity and idolatry.

> Because you have rejected the word of the LORD,
> he has also rejected you from being king.[13]

Rejected you from being king. Samuel wasn't messing around or mincing his message from God here. David was anointed king of Israel shortly after this, and although David had to wait several years (years when God was doing his own work in David's heart) while Saul remained in power, from this point forward, the promise of Saul's rule was effectively done. And Saul knew it. "I have sinned," he said. "I feared the people and obeyed *their* voice."[14] Saul didn't love the people of Israel enough to care more about what God wanted for them (the blessings that come from obedience). Instead, he cared more about what the people wanted from him (the "treasure" of a bit of financial security).

Read that one more time: *Saul didn't love the people of Israel enough to care more about what God wanted for them. He cared more about what the people wanted from him.* He loved their praise, their applause, their five-star reviews of his work as a king. He didn't love them or want what was best for them. His lack of meekness cost him everything.

Then of course we have the apostle Peter. I for one am incredibly thankful for Peter, because his life as recorded in Scripture is evidence that God can use and change people who tend to be too quick to speak and too brash to listen, like me. Peter was a mustang, through and through. Tough to corral and way too fast to speak and act. He was built for the hard life's work of a fisherman and won over by the irresistible draw of Jesus, by the "first look" of his master. Still, his taming took some time. Just like the mustang who resists being changed from wild to gentled, Peter had a tendency to run away in fear. We see that nowhere more clearly than after Jesus' arrest.

Matthew 26:69-75 records Peter denying that he knew Jesus not once, not twice, but three times. When people outside the courtyard where Jesus was being held recognized Peter as one of the arrested man's followers, Peter went so far as to invoke a curse on himself and to swear, "I don't know the man!"[15] In that moment, Peter's fear and his desire for self-preservation won out over his love for Jesus. He wanted the safety of being part of the crowd, and he said whatever he had to in order to get it: "I don't know the man!"

We know that Peter genuinely regretted his denial and that God's plan for Peter's life was not thwarted even by his own self-destruction. In fact, when we read of Peter's boldness and leadership in the early church, it's clear that his repentance from this sin actually emboldened him in a miraculous way. Not only did Peter never again deny knowing Jesus, but he couldn't shut up about him! He was put in jail for preaching the gospel, was supernaturally freed, and went right back into the streets to keep on preaching. When the high priest of Jerusalem said to him, "We gave you strict orders not to teach in [Jesus'] name," Peter said, "We must obey God rather than human beings!"[16] "Sorry, bro," Peter said, "but I don't answer to you because I have no fear of you anymore. I answer to the resurrected King."

Jesus commanded the disciples to go and tell the whole world the gospel, the good news that there is a King so deeply in love with us that he laid down his life and paid the penalty for our sins so that we could enjoy fellowship with the one we were created for forever.[17] The only way that great commission is possible is if we need people less but love them more.

So how do we get there? How do we become the kind of people who are characterized by meekness and not slaves to fear? How do we become love? The answer: self-forgetfulness.

THE REMEDY WE OVERLOOK

In our society today, if someone has low self-esteem, we often remedy this by trying to get them to have higher self-esteem. We tell them, "You are amazing!" or "You are perfect just the way you are!" But is that really what Jesus teaches? Of course, the alternative to this is not the answer either. No one would thrive being told every day, "You're terrible, you know that?" or "You're not good at anything." Feeling overly puffed up or feeling constant shame are equally unhealthy foundations for life. The answer lies outside both of these options. As Timothy Keller says, "Gospel-humility is not thinking more of myself or thinking less of myself, it is *thinking of myself less.*"[18]

The apostle Paul lived out this radically different approach to self-esteem. In his letter to the church in Corinth, he writes, "Now it is required that those who have been given a trust must prove faithful. I care very little if I am judged by you or by any human court; indeed, I do not even judge myself. My conscience is clear, but that does not make me innocent. It is the Lord who judges me." He goes on: "Then you will not be puffed up in being a follower of one of us over against the other. For who makes you different from anyone else? What do you have that you did not receive? And if you did receive it, why do you boast as though you did not?"[19]

We, all of us, are masters in comparison. Our egos are always busy measuring ourselves against others. In fact, I wonder if much of your day, like mine, can easily get caught up in a metrics game, measuring yourself against someone else. Depending on where I think I land along someone else's metric, so lies my self-esteem for the day. We do this with silly things, like who was more productive at work. And we do it with faith, too, like who had a longer, more fruitful quiet time. We even compare things like who had the harder week and thus deserves the weekend rest more. Timothy Keller writes, "The way the normal human ego tries to fill its emptiness and deal with its discomfort is by comparing itself to other people. All the time."[20]

Eugene Peterson paraphrases Paul's passage from 1 Corinthians like this: "For who do you know that really knows *you*, knows your heart? And even if they did, is there anything they would discover in you that you could take credit for? Isn't everything you *have* and everything you *are* sheer gifts from God? So what's the point of all this comparing and competing? You already have all you need. You already have more access to God than you can handle."[21]

We already have all we need. And it's not the respect, admiration, or even the love of other people. In fact, it can be such a trap to care too much about the opinions of others, and an equally damaging trap to set our own standards of goodness. Taking offense is reasonable when something valuable is degraded. However, if we have become lowly in spirit, we will get agitated by true injustice, while insults directed at us will simply roll off our backs. We, like Paul, won't think we're all that great, and we won't have any need to prove otherwise.

We must become desperate for a heart transformed by our Lord into a heart like his, full of purely selfless love. That is the indication of a gospel-humble person, an unoffendable person—because if our ego has been silenced by the awe of God's love, there is no ego to offend. That is true meekness.

And it's possible for all of us to get there.

MEEK MOMENT

Has your ego been getting in the way of your walk with Jesus? Have you fallen into the trap of focusing on others' opinions rather than God's?

Get ready to put this book down, close your eyes, and get quiet. I want you to ask the Lord, *Where have I been choosing fear instead of love?* And then wait. Let the Lord bring something to mind: a person, a situation, a conversation, maybe even a pattern you've ignored.

Now ask him another question: "Jesus, how can I become love in this situation? With this person? In this circumstance?"

Don't just ask what to do—ask who to become.

MURDERER TO MISSIONARY

Remember my missionary friend Carole? She could tell you a hundred stories about the miracles she has seen because of God's indescribable love flowing through her and out to others. She *has* figured out what it means to stop thinking about herself because her thoughts and prayers are so preoccupied with how she can intercede for others. Her story about the day Jacob—a Ugandan rebel—got in the car with her changed the way I see everything.

One day Carole was traveling between Uganda and South Sudan, an eight-hour drive, with some of her staff. They were stopped at the border and were told that they could not go any farther, which was never a good sign, as it all but promised that lawless and violent men were in the area. After a while, the soldiers at the border said, "Okay, you can go, but you have to go in a convoy." They brought military trucks down to escort Carole and her staff. Soon, Carole's team was on the road again. This convoy was not supposed to stop for four hours, but shortly after they got going, they did stop. Two Dinka men in military uniforms—men who were nearly seven feet tall and covered in scars from some of the cultural practices they had—approached the car and let themselves in the back seat on each side of Carole. They announced, "We are your escorts now."

Carole knew exactly what was going to happen. These men were not members of the military. They were rebels with every intention of taking the missionaries off course, raping them, killing them, and then burning the vehicle. Carole knew she was about to die.

But then, almost without thinking, Carole grabbed her Bible and turned to the man on her left. She held it right up to his face, and with all the enthusiasm—*and love*—she could find, she exclaimed to him, "I am so glad you're in the car with me today! What is your name? And have you ever seen one of these before?"

Well, this Dinka soldier, probably twice the size of Carole, was totally caught off guard. Can you imagine? A man used to striking terror in the eyes of everyone he came across was now being accosted by a woman cheerfully trying to get him to talk to her about himself! Likely not what this rebel was expecting. He hesitantly told Carole his name: Jacob.

She jumped right on that. "Jacob! Jacob! Did you know you are in *this* book?" Carole asked as she pounded on the Bible. "In fact, your name is famous in this book! Do you know who Jacob was? Do you know who his father and his grandfather were? Do you know how many kids he had? Oh, let me tell you about his family!" So Carole started in Genesis, enthusiastically going on and on, right in Jacob's face. She went through nearly every Bible story, while Jacob sat and listened, captivated, for three and half hours!

At some point, Jacob put his pistol down. He put his bullets away. It was nothing but the power of God's Word drawing him. Both men in the car began to soften. In fact, as Carole was telling Bible stories about wars and rebellion and the flat-out insane things that people did without God, the men would often stop her, with reactions like "Well, how come they did that?" Everyone in the car would chuckle and smile.

Finally, Carole came to 1 John and started talking about walking in the light and forgiving one another. Jacob began nodding along in understanding, making connections, and he said to Carole, "Oh, that's what our nation needs, isn't it?"

Carole responded, "Yes, Jacob. And that's why I'm here!"

Then Jacob—this large, strong, once-dangerous man—looked Carole right in the eyes and said, "You know, I was going to kill you."

"I know you were," Carole said. "But I have a message stronger than death, and his name is Jesus."

Carole shared the whole gospel with the two Dinka rebels in the car that day. With every ounce of love in her body, she told them the truth, that we are all sinners saved by grace. Three and a half hours had so softened their hearts that they were ready to hear the salvation message. Right there, they prayed with Carole, repented of their sins, and asked Jesus to give them a new heart.

By this time, the convoy was ready to drop the two men off. As Jacob got out of the car, Carole handed him the Bible she had just talked about for nearly four hours on a bumpy, dangerous road in South Sudan. Jacob took it from her, clutching it to his chest like it was worth a million dollars. Carole said, "Jacob, I'm giving you this on one condition: You have to read something every day, and then you have to tell someone else about what you read."

"I will, I promise you!" He smiled.

"Jacob," Carole added, "that makes you a missionary. You got into this car as a murderer, and you got out as a missionary."

This is what love can do.

CHAPTER 10

REST

Come to me, all you who are weary and burdened,
and I will give you rest.
MATTHEW 11:28-30

The first time I walked up to a wild mustang in a round pen, I knew I was looking at an animal who would do anything to break free from the barriers around him. The horse's name was Amarillo (who you know from chapter 1). Remember the missteps I took trying to get that horse to look at me so I could reach out and touch him? He was as strong as he was tense, scratching at the dirt underneath his hooves as if preparing to make a break for it but knowing there was nowhere for him to go other than a few feet in any direction. I could feel Amarillo's restlessness when I approached him. While it took some correction from Grant and some humbling of my posture before I could earn Amarillo's trust,

I really did want the mustang to see me as a safe person. I knew there was something better for him than this life of running aimlessly and anxiously in circles, scared and out of sorts. I knew Amarillo could find a whole new purpose for his strength, if only we could tame him enough to realize it for himself.

In many ways, I think that's true of us and the Lord too. We'd find the truest purpose for our lives if we could humble ourselves enough to trust what *he says* about living.

I see Jesus' words in Matthew 11:28-30 as the anchoring text on meekness in the Bible: "Come to me, all you who are weary and burdened, and I will give you rest. Take my yoke upon you and learn from me, for I am gentle [meek] and humble in heart, and you will find rest for your souls. For my yoke is easy and my burden is light."

We know the heart of Christ is meek: strong yet selfless, powerful yet surrendered, ready and always willing. But I don't want to miss those five words that come before Jesus' description of himself, because I think they are perhaps the biggest blessing that comes from understanding and living out meekness:

I will give you rest.

Rest: the wonderful state of being at peace, at ease, content, and full of faith. Rest is the opposite of fear and anxiety, but today more people than ever before are struggling profoundly with those two things. I know this struggle all too well. So I wonder often if God looks at me and thinks the exact same thing that I did when I saw Amarillo in the round pen: *This spinning and chasing and hustling, this ain't it. This isn't the easy yoke. Come and learn what rest really is.*

THE MODERN CRISIS OF RESTLESSNESS

Let's face it: The world has a big problem. We are radically, dangerously rest-*less*. We are hustling, busying, overscheduling, and distracting ourselves into spiritual oblivion, plagued by information overload and constant comparison along the way.[1] In his poignant book on the concept of hurry, author and pastor John Mark Comer addresses the dangers of a restless life. He writes, "Today, you're far more likely to run into the enemy in the form of an alert on your phone while you're reading your Bible or a multiday Netflix binge or a full-on dopamine addiction to Instagram or a Saturday morning at the office or *another* soccer game on a Sunday or commitment after commitment after commitment in a life of speed. . . . Both sin and busyness have the exact same effect—they cut off your connection to God, to other people, and even to your own soul."[2]

MEEK MOMENT

Take a quick inventory of your week: How much time did you spend really at rest? This will look different for everyone. Rest may be time spent in solitude and prayer, or perhaps it is getting outside for a walk with the Lord or enjoying a good book.

Does your weekly pace look the way you'd like it to, or are you spending more time hustling than experiencing God's presence? Choose today to interrupt the busyness with a moment of rest.

I think of rest as contentment and peace, so I ask myself, *For how much of my week was I truly content?* But even in having to bring up that question, we see part of the problem: We are too busy to pay attention to our own souls. We've got jobs to get to and bills to pay; household projects to finish and TV shows to catch up on. We're busier than ever, working more hours than ever. And we are unhappier than ever.[3]

And in these very things, I consider myself chief among sinners.[4]

HAVE I BUILT SOMETHING MY SOUL CANNOT SUSTAIN?

One morning I sat in a coffee shop, making a call over Zoom for work. On the other side of the screen sat a friend I was partnering with on a project I care deeply about, a project I have put years of work and prayer into. As the call began, we started talking about logistics and a few deadlines we needed to meet to stay on track. I'm not exactly sure what my friend saw—maybe it was a change in my body language or my thoughts growing a bit distant—but she could sense that I had a lot on my mind and finally asked me, "Ryan, you doing okay?"

I thought I was doing okay, honestly. My kids were all doing well. My wife, Annie, was amazing, as always. And work had never been better. So I started telling my friend about all the things I was working on: new filmmaking projects, connections with people I could have only dreamed about meeting years before, growing email lists and follower counts, opportunities for speaking and traveling that only God could orchestrate. My calendar was packed with amazing things. I was on mission, doing what I knew God had called me to do. There were simply a lot of, well, "amazing things" to talk about.

But the more I talked, the more I felt conviction about the commitments I had listed. My true state of low-grade stress slowly started rising to the surface. The feeling was nothing too big or too alarming. And then, out of my own mouth, I voiced a question to my friend that the Holy Spirit had been asking me for weeks but I hadn't said out loud yet: "Have I built something that my soul cannot sustain?"

When I think about that question now, the fact that I didn't know the answer right away *was* the answer. If I am going so hard and so fast—filling my calendar with phone calls and meetings and opportunities that are too good to pass up—that I have to wonder how my own soul is really doing, then I am, without question, going too hard and too fast. I was frantic and anxious in a self-induced way, which is no way to live. And it's also when the most important things in life get left behind.

MEEK MOMENT

You, too, might be asking yourself, *Have I built something my soul cannot sustain?* Maybe it's the mounting bills, the pressure of work, or finding the balance between your marriage, your kids, and your calling. Maybe the relentless pace of life feels like too much. You'll never truly know where the ache in your soul is coming from until you force yourself to pause and examine it. Stop bashing your head against the fence of the round pen, stop running in circles chasing progress but losing peace. Start living with intention. This week, take an afternoon or even just an hour to rest in God's presence.

THE PROBLEM WITH A NOISY LIFE

Modern life has become a steady stream of input. Research tells us that the average person living in the United States checks their phone 205 times a day, approximately every five minutes they are awake. That adds up to spending two and a half months of every year *looking at our phones*. Let that sink in. To add a few more telling statistics, 80.6 percent of people check their phones within ten minutes of waking up, 65.7 percent use their phones while on the toilet, and 53.7 percent have texted with someone in the same room.[5]

And believers are not immune to these realities. Maybe you've been there. The pastor asks you to open your Bible to read this week's passage together, so you pull out your Bible app and follow along. All of a sudden, you're on Instagram, on ESPN, or responding to a text message real quick before you tune in again to the sermon and speaker in front of you. It takes so little to get our minds *off* the things God wants our minds dwelling *on*.

The act of picking up a smartphone is almost unconscious at this point. Our phone is an extra appendage we need to be sure is still there, still part of us. We fill our lives with so many news feeds, catchy videos, contentious comment sections, and the latest "gotta have it" trends that for many of us, our minds are scattered and frenetic before our feet even hit the ground in the morning.

The noise is killing our souls.

We've replaced prayer, reading Scripture, and the discipline of listening with dopamine hits from technology. One requires self-control; the other is an addictive rush of good feelings. As humans, we like our good feelings far too much to exercise a little self-control, especially because these habits appear harmless on the surface. But the constant bombardment of filler noise is anything but harmless. We cannot hear the Holy Spirit if we only hear the people who are the loudest online.

In addition to the dopamine addiction feeding our society, we worship at the altar of efficiency. The "how much can I get done in a twenty-four-hour period in order to feel accomplished?" mindset hovers over us as the final measurement of a successful day. We sleep less, keep twenty-seven tabs open on our computers, and ignore the real people in the room so that we can check off another task. Theologian and author Richard Foster has said, "In contemporary society our Adversary [the devil] majors in three things: noise, hurry, and crowds. If he can keep us engaged in 'muchness' and 'manyness,' he will rest satisfied."[6]

One of the results of the fall of humanity is that we went from people who were made to enjoy prayer, communication, and fellowship with God to people who are too afraid of our own sin to face the presence of a holy God. So instead, we stay busy. Busyness makes it easier to ignore convictions, sidestep sacrifices, and look the other way from the truth. If we never slow down, and if we keep the calendar full, deep down we feel important.

Even for those of us who do pray, who desire to talk to God and ask him for things like safety and health, we talk to God like he's merely a better version of ourselves rather than an entirely holy, completely transcendent, not-to-be-messed-with, and wholly different being entirely. Author and pastor Tyler Staton comments, "God promises peace—a supernatural sort of peace we can't even logically reason out—in place of crippling anxiety. The means of this exchange is prayer . . . [but] even in the church, our prayers don't exchange overwhelmed lives for transcendent peace. They simply drag God into our overwhelmed lives, and the only way we can make him fit is to shrink him down to a reduced size. We keep on praying, but we lower the bar of expectation and power in prayer."[7]

LEARNING TO SURRENDER

One of the biggest and sneakiest lies of the enemy is that real freedom is found in autonomy—in making decisions for our lives independent of anyone else, especially independent of any higher authority with certain expectations of how we are to live. And the enemy's go-to tactic is to make us believe that God is withholding something great from us by giving us limits and rules. He used it in the garden with Adam and Eve when he asked, "Did God *actually* say you can't eat any of the fruit from the tree? Surely he knows that when you do, you'll be like him and know all things, and he's keeping that from you."[8] He tried to use the same tactic to tempt Jesus in the wilderness.

He uses this strategy with us every single day. *Did God really say you shouldn't look at that X-rated website, go partying every weekend, or spend that money on more stuff? Surely he knows you'd be so much happier if you did!* But we don't have to look far to see the fallout from this "more, more, and more" mentality: unprecedented levels of anxiety and depression, personal debt we may never crawl out of, and all manner of preventable health issues. The lie of having no limits, of thinking we are capable of determining for ourselves what our "best life" is, has never been more acceptable—but it remains as toxic as ever.

Surrender is the countercultural invitation of Jesus that helps us fight against Satan's lies. But surrender is not passive. It takes discipline, and discipline is work. Just like a mustang in a round pen, we need to intentionally stop our frantic running long enough to look into the eyes of our Lord. Once we actually slow down and make space for him, that's when he can put on a bridle and a saddle—a yoke, as Jesus might say—which isn't cumbersome, but freeing.[9] The enemy will tell you those limit you, but they don't; they guide you. We are purposeless without them, because if we aren't willing to surrender, God can't take the reins. We are like Agape, the horse with wild eyes, crashing into all sorts of barriers again and again and again.

Everyone wears some sort of yoke; it's the burden of being human in a broken world. But Jesus' yoke is the only one that offers rest.

When I look at Jesus' life and ministry, it always strikes me how chill he was overall. Always a non-anxious presence in the room. Unhurried but on mission. Jesus—who I think we can all agree had much more important work to do than any of us—had time to stop for children, heal a bleeding woman on his way to heal a sick young girl, and finish his commitments in one place before moving on to the next. When word was sent to him to come quickly because one of his dearest companions was sick and likely to die soon, he listened, but then took his time getting there.[10] Everything Jesus did was purposeful and intentional, but it wasn't rushed. And he only had three years to get *all of his public ministry* done! If someone told me I had three years to do all I needed to, I'd be sprinting. Jesus? Nah. He did only what God told him to, and nothing more was needed.

MEEK MOMENT

If you're feeling burned out, take a moment to pray this prayer:

Lord, I ask that you would show me:

Is there anything in my life that's too heavy for my soul to sustain?

Is there anything you want me to quit?

Is there anything you want me to shed?

Is there anything you want me to cast onto you?

And when you whisper your answer, God, help me to act on that guidance today. Not tomorrow or next week, but now. May I find rest for my soul in the obedience to do exactly what you've asked of me, even if it's hard.

Amen.

THE INVITATION TO REST

Rest is not only a good gift from God (that we're not very good at accepting), but it's also a command (that we're not very good at following). It's the fourth of the Ten Commandments: Keep the Sabbath. It's not optional. For those unfamiliar with the term *Sabbath*, it literally means "to rest."[11] It's where we get our English word *sabbatical*, that long break from work most of us wish we could have right now. God could have suggested, "Hey, everyone, you know, it might be a good idea to stop all your work and commitments and just be present to what is right in front of you from time to time," but he did more than that. He's all-knowing, and he obviously knew our human hearts needed something stronger than a kind suggestion.

Keep the Sabbath. Full stop. A command.

As modern Christians, we can tend to breeze past this commandment, largely because of the way the Pharisees made it legalistic. We see Jesus calling out these religious leaders multiple times, at least once directly *about* the Sabbath. The Pharisees had caught Jesus' disciples plucking heads of grain to eat, because can you believe they had the nerve to be hungry on the Sabbath?![12] The Pharisees couldn't. Or, they simply wanted to catch Jesus being wrong about something, anything, which was proving impossible. So they twisted a law that was meant for our good and made it into something they could measure others against. Another metric. Jesus' response? "You don't get it. I'm bigger than all of this. You're missing the whole point."[13]

Honestly, we might be missing the whole point too. We sometimes find ourselves on the other side of the spectrum. *Well, Jesus called out the Pharisees about this, so it's probably not important at all!* That mindset is just as misguided. John Mark Comer explains, "The writer of Hebrews, speaking of Sabbath and its spirit of restfulness, called us to 'make every effort to enter that rest.' Notice the irony of that command; we are to work hard to rest."[14] Because if our bodies never stop to rest—to surrender control—our souls never will either.

If God rested, what on earth makes us think we don't need to?

Sabbath rest is not the only rest we are invited to. Rest is a lifestyle, a posture of faith, and a hallmark of meekness, because living at rest means your heart isn't chasing the temporary but is confident in the eternal, in what Jesus accomplished for us on the cross. I've had to reorient the metrics that held me captive to comparison. Actually, I have to refocus my thoughts, goals, and desires on Jesus all the time, every day, all day. For so long, I thought success looked like growth and achievements. Today, the two standards of success I measure myself by are (1) did I spend time, real time, with the Lord and (2) did I serve someone who can give me nothing? That's it. I work hard, of course. In many ways, I've never been more motivated to creatively get the gospel to everyone I can reach. But I've also never been more aware of how temporary all of this is, how God is the one doing anything of value in me, and how the ways that I rest need to reflect that reality. At 5 p.m., my phone gets put away so that my mind is with my family. I have one of my work team members do all my social media posts, which means that my eyes are on the numbers as little as possible. I make time to pray with my wife every single day; it's a nonnegotiable for us. I'm far from perfect, but I've tasted life with real rest—and I know for sure what life is like without it. Idolizing productivity, and all that accompanies that chase, has stolen enough from me and my family.

These are some of the ways I've been intentional about rest—and I say that because it won't happen if I'm not intentional. I'll say it again: Surrender and rest are not passive. What do you need to do to make room for rest in your life? Limit your screen time or lock your phone up? Ask a friend to be your accountability partner to observe the Sabbath? Take something off your schedule? Say no?

Real rest is about obedience. About taking the easy yoke and working alongside a God who not only doesn't need me to prove anything, but actually *delights* to use me (a mustang like me!) for his Kingdom work. I know in my heart that I'm only going to be at peace when I'm doing his work, not mine. That's rest.

CHAPTER 11

PARTNERSHIP

Working together with him, then, we appeal to you not to receive the grace of God in vain.

2 CORINTHIANS 6:1, ESV

My wife and I have a pool in our backyard, so when Jack, the oldest of our kids, was really little, he wasn't allowed to be outside without supervision. He might have tried to find a way to climb over the pool fence and jump off the diving board to cool off before realizing he didn't know how to get back to the safety of the steps. But as he's gotten older, he hasn't needed that same level of restriction. He not only knows the rule—don't go in the pool without us—but he also knows how to swim. If he ended up in the pool, he could get himself to safety. He's had instruction since his toddler years, and he's grown and learned what's expected, so we trust him more. His two-year-old sister, though? We don't trust her at all out there yet; she's not ready. She is still learning what it means to respect our rules for her and to swap out what she wants for what her mother and I know is best and safe.

This is natural for kids. As they grow, their brains develop, their hearts become more sensitive to right and wrong, and they tend to need less and less correction when it comes to safety and expectations. Parents can, in theory, start to trust their kids with more independence. Eventually, we hope that they become grown men and women who joyfully handle the responsibilities given to them.

Ideally, that's happening with us in our Christian walks too. As we grow in meekness, we get closer to the place where our wills align with the Lord's, and our lives become about co-laboring to tell the world about the saving grace of God.[1] Life becomes a *partnership* with him. It's when you're so in tune with the Lord that you're out of the round pen of life, no longer scared and tense about the good leadership of God, no longer wishing you could run the other way, back to who you were before Jesus changed everything. You're ready for him to move in you, wherever you are, whatever he says.

THE GOAL ALL ALONG

Christians often talk about the idea of having a personal relationship with God, whether that's being a friend of God, a child of God, or a disciple of Jesus. And the Bible clearly presents our relationship with God as all of these things. He is the most perfect relationship we *could* have because he meets our needs as all of these things: Friend, Father, Teacher, and Savior.

But there's another way the Bible talks about our relationship with God that doesn't get quite as much airtime in the church, and that's a *partnership*: working alongside him to accomplish a goal together.[2] God wants to bring the gospel to the ends of the earth *with* us. He wants to use us in our homes, our workplaces, our neighborhoods, wherever our feet are, *as we are*, to be part of his mission to bring the gospel to the ends of the earth. And partnership was his plan from the beginning.

In Genesis 1, we see that God created a good world full of promise and opportunity for fellowship with him, and then he appointed humans as his partners in bringing about more flourishing in the world. But the challenge quickly becomes obvious: The human heart is not robotic, programmed to a default mode of obedience. If there were no other choice but to obey, that wouldn't be love. Giving someone else only one choice is a demand, not a kindness. The human heart gets to choose, and too often we don't seem to want to partner with God. In Genesis 3, the first humans, Adam and Eve, rebelled. They thought there was something better for them outside the limits God placed on them, so they broke those limits and broke a relationship in the process.

I want to be clear here. Even though we—you and me and the rest of the world—were not there in the beginning of time, we all have the same problem as the first man and woman God created: sin and selfishness. Not to mention an obvious tendency to second-guess God's goodness in favor of our own judgment. Maybe I wasn't the first one to take the bite of the fruit God told me not to touch, but I'm guilty of that same kind of sin a thousand times over. I *would* have taken the bite. Yes, I'm talking about history, but I'm also telling you with confidence that throughout history and still today, we have a hard time partnering with God.

So God sent his Son to be the perfect partner that we are meant to embody, despite often failing to. Through Jesus, partnership with God is available to anyone. His sacrifice on the cross allows us to return to him again and again. And again.

Jesus wants to partner with us. And he knows that, in order to do so, we need his help. On our own, we will stay wild and rebellious. This is why Jesus is the most committed and steadfast mustang tamer of all time. He's going to show up to the round pen every single day to prove to us that he is worth trusting. No one has ever or could ever be more dedicated to transforming us from restless and lost people into partners who increasingly reflect his character as we live on mission with him.

DYLAN'S STORY

The longer I follow Jesus, the clearer it becomes that partnering with him is going to look different for everyone. Most of us, if we are honest, want our life of co-laboring with the Lord to be "blessed and highly favored" *because* we are working with him.[3] The common thought is *I follow Jesus, so life should be good.* But that's not always what the relationship looks like. In fact, I'm starting to think the toughest assignments and the most trying situations in this life are given to the strongest, most loyal mustangs, the ones the Lord knows can be trusted with faith-testing circumstances. That's how I feel about my good friend Dylan Mandell.

Dylan is a twenty-one-year-old who *gets* what it means to partner with the Lord to bring the gospel to everyone. When Dylan was a senior in high school, he was diagnosed with a rare cancer in his jaw. In order for doctors to remove the tumor, he underwent a massive surgery that involved such a difficult recovery that there were moments Dylan didn't know if he would breathe on his own again. But he fought hard, leaned on his faith, and recovered. He went off to college at Texas Christian University (TCU), hoping cancer was a thing of the past.

It wasn't. A year later, doctors found more cancer, and another surgery ensued, this one even more difficult than the first—not only because of the complexity of the surgery but also because of the traumatic memories that came with it. Doctors had to remove Dylan's fibula (the smaller bone next to the shin) and pieces of his quad muscle to help rebuild parts of his face where more cancer was taken out. At this point, a fit, athletic young man, so full of life and potential, was having his whole body torn apart to try to save his life.

It was also at this point that Dylan had to get real clear with the Lord about what the purpose of his suffering was.

"My first desire was to know the truth," Dylan said when sharing his story with me. "These trials didn't just happen for no reason, so I needed to find out what the purpose was. And I think the purpose was, honestly, to find my faith through suffering. To understand there is a God who loves us so much, and that it breaks his heart to allow trials but he knows the fruit that can come from overcoming."

These are words that, unless they come from someone who knows the kind of suffering Dylan knows, can feel like platitudes. But when you hear them from the mouth of someone who has truly faced death, you understand in a powerful way that they aren't platitudes. To trust God to produce fruit out of suffering is to believe in a vital truth about his character: that he *will* complete the good work he started in us, no matter what.[4] Dylan is a young man who knows that when you're in the valley, at the bottom, out of options and hope, the only thing that bolsters you and encourages you to hold your head up enough to see the next inch forward is the truth.

"When you're crying out to God in a low moment, he's there with you," Dylan told me in a choked-up voice. "He's there whispering, 'I'm sorry; I'm with you, but you don't know now what you will.'"[5]

Dylan's words reflect what Paul says in Romans 5: "We rejoice in our sufferings, knowing that suffering produces endurance, and endurance produces character, and character produces hope, and hope does not put us to shame, because God's love has been poured into our hearts through the Holy

Spirit who has been given to us."[6] Notice that Paul writes, "We rejoice *in* our sufferings."[7] That's very different from rejoicing *for* them. We don't have to rejoice when the diagnosis comes, when the phone rings with bad news, or when our plans crumble. No, that's not biblical at all. But because of Jesus, because of the hope he has given us that will not disappoint, we can still rejoice *in the midst* of grief, of loss, of death. We can still be on mission as God's partners.

With the second surgery behind him, Dylan once again met the challenge of intense physical recovery: relearning to eat, walk, and live fully. When he was able, Dylan started getting up at 3 a.m. to do what most of us would label "insane" workouts in his garage. He was totally focused on surviving cancer and being stronger than he'd ever been, even without a fibula and part of a quad. After pushing himself to the limit physically, he would spend as much of the rest of the day as he could in communion with the Lord, reading Scripture, begging to see more of Jesus in his circumstances with each passing day. He went back to TCU, returned to his classes and his social circle, and was looking forward to moving on with the rest of his college life.

But that cancer wouldn't quit. A year later, Dylan got the news that not only was the cancer back, but it had spread to his lungs and lymph nodes, moving his prognosis from grim to terminal. Dylan took the news with such peace that even the doctor, a seasoned oncologist, couldn't believe his demeanor. But instead of accepting the prognosis, Dylan's mindset was "Cancer Round Three: Let's Go." And the same fighting spirit Dylan had shown over the last three years eventually carried him into a miraculous season of remission. One that everyone around him believed would stick.

I was with Dylan, who I've come to love and consider a brother, when he got the email with the results that his cancer was back for the fourth time. Dylan had been sure this part of his story was behind him, that God was doing in him the miracle that he had begged him to do for many years. Dylan thought that he would be celebrating giving God the glory and that a miraculous healing would be his testimony.

Instead, he found out, "You've still got two tumors on your lungs."

Dylan went straight to his backyard and fell to his knees in tear-filled prayer. His grief was all-consuming, and there was nothing anyone could do to slow the waves of sadness and disappointment hitting him over and over. He'd been so expectant for healing. Everyone who knew his story was expectant too. Now Dylan had to hold the reality that his expectations were not what God had for him in that moment. He had to come back into alignment with God's will for his life, even though it wasn't what he wanted.

Some of us might read Dylan's story and wonder, *Why would God be so cruel? Just to teach someone a lesson? Aren't there any other ways to refine one's character?* The problem of evil has been a barrier to faith in Jesus for people throughout human history. "How could a good God allow suffering?" is an honest question. And it's one God is not afraid of. You can ask him your toughest, most painful questions. David's laments to the Lord in the psalms should give you not only a precedent but permission:

> How long, Lord? Will you forget me forever?
>   How long will you hide your face from me?
> How long must I wrestle with my thoughts
>   and day after day have sorrow in my heart?
>   How long will my enemy triumph over me?
>
> PSALM 13:1-2

> My God, my God, why have you forsaken me?
>   Why are you so far from saving me,
>   so far from my cries of anguish?
> My God, I cry out by day, but you do not answer,
>   by night, but I find no rest.
>
> PSALM 22:1-2

Dylan has had no shortage of lamenting moments. A life of partnership with God doesn't mean we won't ever have questions or sadness. But it does mean God has graciously given us an eternal perspective that we can return to in the most devastating moments. It means we cling to the things we know are true and live boldly from there. For Dylan, it meant this: "I knew that [my diagnosis] wasn't really life or death. It was life or life. Life or death was done for me when I put my faith in Jesus."[8]

At the time of this writing, Dylan is fighting cancer for the fourth time. No one knows what God is going to do, but we all know Dylan is going to continue being the warrior he has always been for each and every day that God gives him. And he is going to keep telling anyone who will listen that God is good, big, and better than anything the world could offer. Dylan is unattached to the world, to the things most of us chase. He's had everything stripped away, and he has responded only by wanting to honor Jesus. You can't tempt him with fame. You can't offend him. He's in this fight for God's glory, and he's surrendered the ending in favor of living every day with the Lord. Jesus tells us that his yoke is easy and his burden is light, because he knows that life is going to be hard for everyone in some measure. The yoke Dylan carries, as impossible as it seems to those of us watching, is a burden he holds with steadfastness and faith because of the Savior who bears it with him. There are a handful of people in my life who I can look at and say, "Yeah, that person reflects the character of God. He looks like Jesus." That's the *first* thing I would say about Dylan.

THE MEEK WILL INHERIT THE EARTH

In the middle of Jesus' most famous sermon, the Sermon on the Mount, he gives the crowd listening a list of blessings, which we call the beatitudes. In that list, Jesus flips worldly wisdom and counsel on its head with his directions on how we are to live: being poor in spirit, hungering for righteousness, being merciful and pure in heart.[9] But he also says this statement—words that could change everything if we learned to live them out: "Blessed are the meek, for they will inherit the earth."[10]

Inherit the earth? What does that mean? Are meek people written into God's final will with some kind of massive treasure in store? Yes, actually, but the treasure doesn't have anything to do with money or power. There is a lot of rich biblical scholarship on the interpretation of that sentence about meekness, but what we know for sure is that if Jesus said it, he means for us to take it seriously. First, to *be* meek, and, second, to *trust* that we will be recipients of his promises in return.

Psalm 37 can help us get a little deeper and attempt to tie together the tapestry of meekness we've examined in this book. In verse 11, King David, the author of this psalm, writes, "The meek will inherit the land and enjoy peace and prosperity." Jesus knew this verse when he reiterated it in the Sermon on the Mount, and it is almost a perfect parallel. He also would have known the additional context this psalm gives about meekness. Before Psalm 37:11, we read,

> Commit your way to the Lord;
>   trust in him and he will do this:
> He will make your righteous reward shine like the dawn,
>   your vindication like the noonday sun.
>
> Be still before the Lord,
>   and wait patiently for him;

do not fret when people succeed in their ways,
when they carry out their wicked schemes.

Refrain from anger and turn from wrath;
do not fret—it leads only to evil.

PSALM 37:5-8

In these verses, God lays out a vision of meekness, of a Christ follower seeking to know the heart of Jesus. John Piper summarizes the vision like this:

> Meekness begins when we put our trust in God. Then, because we trust him, we commit our way to him. We roll onto him our anxieties, our frustrations, our plans, our relationships, our jobs, our health. And then we wait patiently for the Lord. We trust his timing and his power and his grace to work things out in the best way for his glory and for our good. . . .
>
> *Meekness begins with God and ends with God.* And therefore whenever we see a person like that, we give God the glory.[11]

Meekness *is* the wild mustang—powerful and strong, capable of striking fear into its challengers but made gentle by the power of the Holy Spirit and the new heart offered to those who trust in Jesus by grace through faith. The mustang is always listening to the nudges of his leader. But being tamed and gentled doesn't make a mustang lose his strong and bold nature; it simply brings it under loving submission. A truly meek person has been tamed and gentled into a life that looks different from everyone around them because their mission is no longer their own—it's God's. We are his partners, moving in the power of the Holy Spirit, part of a plan and purpose that is more than we could have ever asked for or imagined.

There is no better pursuit for your life than that.

MEEK MOMENT

I want to invite you into something deeper than the way you've been living. I want to invite you into a rhythm of communion with the Lord. A rhythm of hearing his still, small voice and enjoying his presence more than anything else in the world. A life of obedience, contentment, rest in God's sovereignty, and confidence in his purposes for you.

Meekness will be the greatest gift of your life. Or maybe I should say it this way: The fruit of meekness will be the greatest dividend you'll ever receive. The paradox of it—the rest for your soul and the adventure you'll go on—will continually blow your mind as you yield to the Lord's leadership. So find a time, every single day, to come into his presence. Create a habit of asking him for permission, inviting him into your decisions, learning the nudge of his reins, and anticipating where he wants to go next. Because as you do, I believe you—and your brothers and sisters around the world—will inherit the earth and advance the Kingdom.

My hope and prayer is for you to see what God can do with a wild heart when it is finally surrendered to him. For you to treasure the presence of Jesus more than anything. To feel stronger than ever because you are being guided by the gentle hands of your Creator.

And to live the rest of your life pursuing the heart of Jesus, meek as a mustang.

ACKNOWLEDGMENTS

This book could not have been written without the Lord's merciful pruning. In his kindness, God allowed me to walk through seasons of wilderness, experiencing what felt like failure, humiliation, and long stretches of waiting. Looking back now, I am deeply grateful. He was shaping more than a message; he was shaping me.

Then he gave me my sweet Annie, a wife who patiently prayed, encouraged, and loved me as a true partner in every sense. Thank you, baby. Your constant faith and quiet strength are more than I could have asked for or imagined in a wife.

And to my beautiful children, Jack, Lucy, Hallie, and Peter, I would not so fully understand the heart of a father's love without you. My prayer is that one day you will read this book and fall even more in love with Jesus and his beautiful heart of meekness.

I'd also like to thank Carly Kellerman at Alive Literary Agency, and the team at Tyndale, for believing in this message, helping to shape it, and taking a chance on me to steward these words and stories.

To God be the glory, always.

NOTES

INTRODUCTION

1. Matthew 5:5.
2. Matthew 11:29, KJV.
3. See Luke 4:1-13.
4. See Matthew 21:12-13.
5. See Matthew 26:53, 62-63.

CHAPTER 1: IT'S YOUR RELATIONSHIP

1. See Ephesians 3:20-21.
2. See Romans 2:4.
3. Bill Johnson, "Seeing the Eyes of a Loving Father," sermon, posted March 22, 2022, by Bill Johnson Teaching (Official), YouTube, https://www.youtube.com/watch?v=yI67pDL0iMM.
4. See 1 Peter 2:9.
5. See Luke 11:53.
6. See 2 Corinthians 12:9.

CHAPTER 2: WHY WOULD YOU WANT A MUSTANG?

1. "With 1 Million Leaving the Church Every Year, Is Gen Z the Faithless Generation?" *Sojourners,* February 26, 2024, https://sojo.net/articles/sponsored/1-million-leaving-church-every-year-gen-z-faithless-generation.
2. See Mark 1:16-20; Matthew 4:18-22; Luke 5:2-11; John 1:40-42.
3. Timothy Keller with Kathy Keller, *The Meaning of Marriage: Facing the Complexities of Commitment with the Wisdom of God* (Penguin, 2011), 48.
4. See Mark 3:17.
5. Matthew 9:11-12.
6. Luke 15:1-2.

7. Strong's #4327—προσδέχομαι," StudyLight.org, accessed February 18, 2026, https://www.studylight.org/lexicons/eng/greek/4327.html.
8. See Luke 15:3-7.
9. See Luke 15:8-10.
10. Luke 15:17.
11. See Luke 15:11-20.
12. Matthew Williams, "The Prodigal Son's Father Shouldn't Have Run!" *Biola Magazine*, May 31, 2010, https://www.biola.edu/blogs/biola-magazine/2010/the-prodigal-sons-father-shouldnt-have-run.
13. Genesis 3:1.
14. Keller, *Meaning of Marriage,* 48.
15. See Exodus 2–4.
16. See Exodus 14:19-31.
17. See Joshua 2.
18. See 1 Samuel 13:14.
19. See Acts 9.

CHAPTER 3: THE BIT IN THE MOUTH

1. See 1 Chronicles 22.
2. See Luke 9:51-55.
3. 2 Samuel 6:22.
4. See John 13:23.
5. See Philippians 1:21-24.
6. Matthew 16:23.
7. John 18:1-11.
8. See Matthew 5:9.
9. See 1 Samuel 13:14.

CHAPTER 4: THE NUDGE OF THE REINS

1. "Strong's #26—ἀγάπη," StudyLight.org, accessed February 23, 2026, https://www.studylight.org/lexicons/eng/greek/26.html.
2. "Strong's #5373—φιλία," StudyLight.org, accessed February 23, 2026, https://www.studylight.org/lexicons/eng/greek/5373.html.
3. "What Is *Eros* Love?" Got Questions, accessed February 23, 2026, https://www.gotquestions.org/eros-love.html.
4. "Strong's #5387—φιλόστοργος," StudyLight.org, accessed February 23, 2026, https://www.studylight.org/lexicons/eng/greek/5387.html.
5. Augustine, *Confessions*, trans. Carolyn J.-B. Hammond (Harvard University Press, 2014), 1.1.
6. See 1 Samuel 23:1-5, 10-11, 12-14; 30:8-9; 2 Samuel 2:1-2; 5:17-25; 21:1.

7. 1 Samuel 30:4.
8. 1 Samuel 30:8.
9. 1 Samuel 30:8.
10. See 1 Samuel 30:9-31.
11. See John 2:1-12.
12. See Matthew 9:20-22.
13. See Luke 5:18-25.
14. Jamie Winship, "The Kidnapping Case That Changed Everything," interview by Josh Doyle, posted December 23, 2025, by No Longer Nomads, YouTube, https://www.youtube.com/watch?v=i7_SPcUA7BM.
15. Maryam Rostampour and Marziyeh Amirizadeh, *Captive in Iran: A Remarkable True Story of Hope and Triumph amid the Horror of Tehran's Brutal Evin Prison* (Tyndale House Publishers, 2013).
16. Ryan Miller, host, *The Jesus People Podcast*, season 1, episode 1, "Episode 1 of *The Jesus People Podcast*—Compton Mayor Aja Brown," September 14, 2024, https://podcasts.apple.com/us/podcast/episode-1-of-the-jesus-people-podcast-compton-mayor/id1768632876?i=1000669603169.
17. Miller, *Jesus People Podcast*, "Compton Mayor Aja Brown."
18. Miller, *Jesus People Podcast*, "Compton Mayor Aja Brown."
19. See 2 Chronicles 14:1-7.
20. 2 Chronicles 14:11.
21. 2 Chronicles 16:7.
22. See 2 Chronicles 16:10.
23. 2 Chronicles 16:12.
24. See 2 Samuel 5:18-25.
25. John 10:27, ESV.

CHAPTER 5: HIDDEN AND HOLY

1. ESV, emphasis mine.
2. Luke 9:53, ESV.
3. Luke 9:54, ESV.
4. See Luke 9:55.
5. See Mark 3:17.
6. See John 3:30.
7. See Acts 12:1-2.
8. Dan Braga, "Technically, a Brand Is a Burn Scar," *Seeing Sparrows*, Substack, October 13, 2025, https://danbraga.substack.com/p/technically-a-brand-is-a-burn-scar?utm_campaign=post&utm_medium=email&triedRedirect=true.
9. Mark 1:22, 28, ESV.

10. Mark 1:33, ESV.
11. See Mark 1:35.
12. See Mark 1:37.
13. Mark 1:38, ESV, emphasis mine.
14. Zack Eswine, *The Imperfect Pastor: Discovering Joy in Our Limitations Through a Daily Apprenticeship with Jesus* (Crossway, 2015), 26.

CHAPTER 6: YOUR FEAR IS ACTUALLY YOUR PRIDE

1. See Exodus 3:11; 4:13.
2. Exodus 3:7-8, 10.
3. See Matthew 23:12.
4. See 1 Peter 5:7.
5. See Philippians 4:6; Matthew 6:25-34; 1 Peter 5:7.
6. See Acts 4:23-31.
7. See John 15:18.
8. To learn more, read Elisabeth Elliot, *Through Gates of Splendor* (Tyndale House Publishers, 2024).

CHAPTER 7: THE GRACE OF THE WILDERNESS

1. Danny Goodwin, "How Long Will People Wait for Websites to Load in 2024? Survey Says . . . ," Search Engine Land, August 15, 2024, https://searchengineland.com/people-wait-website-load-2024-stat-445223.
2. ESV, emphasis mine.
3. Exodus 17:3, ESV.
4. See Exodus 17:4.
5. Timothy Keller with Kathy Keller, *The Meaning of Marriage: Facing the Complexities of Commitment with the Wisdom of God* (Penguin, 2011), 48.
6. Psalm 51:1-4, 10-12, emphasis mine.
7. See Philippians 4:8-9.
8. See Exodus 33:15.
9. Deuteronomy 32:51-52, CSB.
10. Deuteronomy 34:10-12.

CHAPTER 8: THE GRACE OF THE WILDERNESS

1. "Stong's #4239—πραΰς," StudyLight.org, accessed March 6, 2026, https://studylight.org/lexicons/eng/greek/4239.html.
2. "The Power of Meekness," Life in Abundance, September 23, 2021, https://lifeinabundance.com/the-power-of-meekness/.
3. "Do what thou wilt" is the central, foundational tenet of Thelema, a spiritual philosophy established by Aleister Crowley in 1904; "What is the

central tenet of Thelema?" Bible Hub, accessed February 25, 2026, https://biblehub.com/q/what_is_the_central_tenet_of_thelema.htm.
4. Philippians 1:3-4, emphasis mine.
5. Philippians 1:27.
6. Philippians 2:3, emphasis mine.
7. Luke 10:17.
8. Luke 10:18.
9. Luke 10:20.
10. See Matthew 10:39.
11. Philippians 1:21.
12. Revelation 12:11, CSB.
13. Matthew Henry, *Matthew Henry's Commentary on the Whole Bible*, vol. 6, *Acts to Revelation*, (MacDonald Publishing Company, 1970), 1161, emphasis mine.

CHAPTER 9: UNOFFENDABLE

1. "About Carole Ward," Favor International, accessed February 23, 2026, https://www.favorintl.org/about/our-story/founder.
2. Ryan Miller, host, *The Jesus People Podcast*, season 1, episode 27, "African Missionary: Tear Down Strongholds and Conquer Fear," July 14, 2025, https://podcasts.apple.com/us/podcast/episode-27-the-jesus-people-podcast-african/id1768632876?i=1000717267140.
3. My interview with Carole Ward on *The Jesus People Podcast* remains one of the most impactful interviews I've ever done. I give the highlights in this chapter, but it's worth a listen.
4. Timothy Keller, *The Freedom of Self-Forgetfulness: The Path to True Christian Joy* (10Publishing, 2012), 43.
5. Edward T. Welch, *When People Are Big and God Is Small: Overcoming Peer Pressure, Codependency, and the Fear of Man* (P&R Publishing, 2023), 20, emphasis my own.
6. Welch, *When People Are Big*, 23.
7. Welch, *When People Are Big*, 30.
8. 1 Samuel 15:3, ESV.
9. 1 Samuel 15:9, ESV.
10. See 1 Samuel 15:13.
11. See 1 Samuel 15:14-15.
12. 1 Samuel 15:16, ESV.
13. I Samuel 15:22-23, ESV.
14. 1 Samuel 15:24, ESV, emphasis mine.
15. Matthew 26:74.

16. Acts 5:28-29.
17. See Matthew 28:19-20; John 3:16.
18. Keller, *Freedom of Self-Forgetfulness*, 32, emphasis mine.
19. 1 Corinthians 4:2-4, 6-7.
20. Keller, *Freedom of Self-Forgetfulness*, 17.
21. 1 Corinthians 4:7-8, MSG.

CHAPTER 10: REST

1. "Spiritual oblivion" is a term borrowed from Ronald Rolheiser in his book *The Holy Longing: The Search for a Christian Spirituality* (Penguin Random House, 2014), 32.
2. John Mark Comer, *The Ruthless Elimination of Hurry: How to Stay Emotionally Healthy and Spiritually Alive in the Chaos of the Modern World* (Crown Publishing Group, 2019), 20.
3. Comer, *Ruthless Elimination of Hurry.*
4. See 1 Timothy 1:15.
5. Chandra Steele, "Yikes! The Average American Spent 2.5 Months on Their Phone in 2024," *PCMag*, December 27, 2024, https://www.pcmag.com/articles/yikes-the-average-american-spent-25-months-on-their-phone-in-2024.
6. Richard J. Foster, *The Celebration of Discipline: The Path to Spiritual Growth* (HarperCollins, 2009), 15.
7. Tyler Staton, *Praying Like Monks, Living Like Fools: An Invitation to the Wonder and Mystery of Prayer* (HarperCollins, 2022), 13, 18.
8. My paraphrase of Genesis 3:1, 5.
9. He actually did say exactly that in Matthew 11:28-30.
10. See John 11.
11. "Sabbath," Bible Study Tools, accessed February 24, 2026, biblestudytools.com/dictionary/sabbath/.
12. See Matthew 12:1-2.
13. My paraphrase of Matthew 12:3-8.
14. Comer, *Ruthless Elimination of Hurry*, 150.

CHAPTER 11: PARTNERSHIP

1. See 1 Corinthians 3:9.
2. The Bible Project has an excellent video diving deeper into this topic on partnership and covenants. I highly recommend it: Whitney Woollard, "The Five Key Covenants God Makes with Humans in the Bible," Bible Project, April 4, 2018, https://bibleproject.com/articles/covenants-the-backbone-bible/.

3. See Luke 1:28.
4. See Philippians 1:6.
5. Ryan Miller, host, *The Jesus People Podcast*, season 1, episode 17, "Dylan Mandell: From a 'Terminal' Diagnosis to Unstoppable Faith," https://podcasts.apple.com/us/podcast/episode-17-the-jesus-people-podcast-dylan-mandell/id1768632876?i=1000698965003.
6. Romans 5:3-5, ESV.
7. Emphasis mine.
8. Miller, *Jesus People Podcast*, "Dylan Mandell."
9. See Matthew 5:3-10.
10. Matthew 5:5.
11. John Piper, "Blessed Are the Meek," Desiring God, February 9, 1986, https://www.desiringgod.org/messages/blessed-are-the-meek, emphasis mine.

ABOUT THE AUTHORS

RYAN MILLER is an online evangelist, author, filmmaker, and founder of The Jesus People, a digital ministry reaching millions of people each year with the gospel through social media, podcasts, documentaries, and daily Scripture-centered content. With a heart for helping people encounter the presence of God in real and transformative ways, Ryan blends sound biblical teaching with practical spiritual formation for everyday life.

Ryan is the host of *The Jesus People Podcast*, where he engages pastors, theologians, influencers, and everyday believers in conversations about faith, suffering, redemption, and revival. He is also a documentary producer behind multiple faith-based film projects that spotlight persecuted Christians, modern-day miracles, and radical testimonies of life change.

In addition, Ryan founded Share the Struggle, a Christian mental health platform providing Scripture-based encouragement, coaching, and resources to help people walk through anxiety, shame, and emotional pain with hope and faith. His writing and teaching consistently point readers back to the authority of Scripture, the power of the Holy Spirit, and the freedom found in surrendering fully to Jesus.

Ryan lives in Texas with his wife, Annie, and their four young children. When he's not creating content or traveling for ministry, he enjoys family life, cheering on the San Diego Padres, and finding the best burritos around. Connect with Ryan through *The Jesus People Podcast* and The Jesus People online.

KATIE M. KELLEY is a writer, teacher, lifelong learner, and mom to six amazing kids. She is the author of *Gluing the Cracks* and *Grace Will Be There*. Katie is also a contributing writer and podcast cohost at Coffee + Crumbs, and her writing has been featured on The Gospel Coalition, Risen Motherhood, Journeywomen, MomCo, Motherly, and more. When she's not finding time in the margins of her day to put words on the page, she's either making someone a snack, cleaning up a mess, or riding the Peloton.